Claud

The Other Side
of Where I
Used to Live

An A.C.C.E.S.S. Art Production

ISBN- 978-0-6151-7698-7 paperback

This book was edited and published at

A.C.C.E.S.S. Art Corp. International

157 Butler Street, New Bedford, Massachusetts 02744

Visit our website: www.accessartcorpintl.org

"The artistic and cultural community of educators, shipmates, and supporters"

*Poetry **is** the revolution.*
Each voice rises
equal to be heard.

"love calls us to the things
of this world"
Richard Wilbur

This book is dedicated to Thomas Alan Grace,
Captain of my true course, for his love and devoted
support.

Contents

PREFACE

Postmodern experience is a cauldron of emotion and intelligence
underscored by chemical invention. Nuclear fusion/fission
of the hemispheres of the brain and so division of the spirit--
psychometry of material energies explained and naturalized--
experimentation with brain waves-experiments toward a 'flat planet'--
cloning--our age has observed remarkable exploits
with space and time similar to ancient alchemical explorations.
Our common sea, earth, air, fire are not the only elements at
our disposal in creating our sacraments and rituals. Tears
of sorrow and joy, salt, blood, our original acquaintances which
stir emotions and visualizations now give way to gas, ethers,
military poisons, toxic environmental substances.

Contemporary literature, theatrical poetry, poetry itself,
must serve as signifier of these digressions between faith and
technology, these leaps between matter and spirit. This aesthetic
sometimes deserves numbers, lists, spaces of silence between these
colliding rhythms rather than words. A montage of this order
would do justice to the quantitative, impersonal aspect of this
idiom. The bones and tombs of the dead, the imaginations of
the living calling in urgent voice to affect redemption and
transformation of our time, reveal our personal will and
vision dedicated to the task. Desire and empowerment --these two
functions strive to recreate the world, to establish reality and to oust
the outmoded institutions and refuges which are our modus operandi,

a superficial media, the seductions of chemical products and drugs, fashion and style which are our trajectories toward oblivion. These are not deep culture and their roots are anchored in an ancient diabolical reality. The individualism of the American spirit struggles for an interior life and attempts to grab this from the empty space offered by these contemporary stabs at solutions. We share many voices, many idioms, diverse modes in an effort to program history and ourselves. The distillation of these communal bonds embraces us in the progression of the human spirit. We can research the news, the mastheads, to interpret and rend life insignificant or render it beatific. The artist who gives permission for the incorporation of balance in the work saves the culture. The artistic creation is not only a symbol, a central image, but instead an echo of voices, of spaces, of quantum leaps of reality. Cause-and-effect, physical and biochemical analyses, and dialectic are all resolved in a Living Idea. Microcosm and macrocosm join in the rhythm, the word.

Language is a way of sculpting breath. Articulations like these demand the full participation of our presence--and our breath, our rhythm, the infusion of our spirit is central in our effort to understand and decode the message of the holy spirit living in our world. Both inspiration and expiration are grounded spirit and intelligence of the Poet who is standard-bearer of the flag on a new, flexible, and free frontier.....

FORWARD!

I have chosen to focus the principles set forth in the preface of this book around my experiential contact with New Bedford, Massachusetts. It is my hometown…as much as I have a hometown. There are those who know New Bedford for its past as the foremost whaling port on the planet. It was "the City that lit the world" with export of its whale oil, and its Whaling Museum demonstrates the crucial influence of both the city and the industry on global development.

Others recall its textile industry and the generations of mill workers clothing the nation, exporting beyond our borders. The city's "New Bedford Tech" textile college became Southeastern Massachusetts University, and has now advanced into a University of Massachusetts campus. The textile department, once lulled into quietude by the factory hegira South, now once again hums with promise.

New Bedford currently is known as "the richest fishing port in the country". It isn't the largest, but the active fishing industry has made it the wealthiest producer. As fishing has been increasingly restricted over the past twenty years, some fishermen have bemoaned their fate and turned to 'retraining', shipping out, or substances.

New Bedford has been trying for more than a decade to improve the quality of life here while redefining itself for the future. The momentum toward heritage tourism has been amplified by the efforts of the museums, the theaters, and the sprouting cultural groups. We have opened the studios of numerous artists working in affordable urban lofts, offered monthly free events at multiple venues, and clusters of classes in everything from new media to ethnic cuisine. The abundant ethnic mix here amplifies the diversified history of the City, necessarily attracting an international maritime labor pool. The Portuguese dominate the cultural marketplace: there are more Portuguese and Cape Verdeans here than in their respective nations. The bakeries, cafes, clubs, and media which cater to them can be enjoyed by those who've moved to the suburbs.

Yet we are still an underserved city: there are those who work long hours and have no 'leisure', those whose drug culture has supplanted their ethnic impulse, and the urban thug culture of inner city transplants looking for a way out of the ghetto.

These characters, images, lines, references are here in this book because they are part of life lived, or its other side. We all have "where we used to live" and that place had "an other side"; indeed, it had many facets. The other side is not necessarily dark underworld , but it can be. It is the point of view we could never realize while we were embedded in our reality; it is only by moving away from it that we can see the multiple layers, masks, worlds.

I'll take you there, if you allow me, in these time capsules. You'll see bits of New Orleans, Boston, Puerto Rico, and Québec filtered through my lens where the waterfront dominates and the struggle to survive is intertwined with the triumph in so doing.

October 28, 2007

the muse in blazes

Anthem

I'm as light as a feather
I'll last forever

I'm as light as a feather
I'll dance forever

the girl-child swings
into the sun, chanting
the anthem of her People...

she spins out in circles
the coiled rope dangling
from the oak like a snake
unwinding with the precision
of a compass needle,
magnetized by ground
kicked by small feet expecting
eternity
to behold with reverence
the beloved shield of the ancestors
traced on the earth.

Spiraling toward noon,
she winds against the clock's momentum
gathering in a sweep the divided heart
from the corners of the world.
This is the way the world was made.
The People call it the dance of the turtles.

Québeçois folk-poet as child

with my skirt in my hands I danced
whirling white, like that
there is no grass, no ground
My feet were so small
I never touched down
...on ripples of my mother's
guitar
white water
Indian waters...
Nahanie, I'm an Indian river
I'm a tribe
my mother told me
I'm a chord she fingered
I'm my father's rhythm
If I follow these steps
it is not my own doing
If I dance
it's the grace of this place
that cradles me like light
A bird
folds in his wings against the night--
I raised to my face my dress
to hide my pride
white moon on dusky thighs
and laugh, delighted
running the Plains of Abraham
low as the mountain curled in the sky

Brackets of My Education

Doc   for Evariste LaRivière

"dada doc " I learned to speak
like the rhythm of hearts you monitored-you moved
your office from the Avenue to the top of our hill-
I played with your stethoscope, violin,
and pipes and helped you mix
stomach powders or label the magic
"white medicine" that scared chest colds away-
You were schooled in the town I was born in
and taught me the fine French here in America-
they said you brought half the North End
into this world--I counted the endless procession
of hats that came to your wake as I leaned from the
banister watching--
today I heal with metaphor and beat of breath,
and while people gave you fruit of their gardens,
I get stories and poems filled with all the complaints and
growth that you taught me was life.

Flore

You tucked that child's violin under your chin
but stopped playing when your mama died
forgoing children for career, you were my pioneer
female doctor of the Jacques Building
using your family name for decades
after marriage, after your Boston education
(one of three women in your day)
I'd climb into your high chair and try on the goggles
of lenses you'd fit on your downtown clients--at play
I used your glove stretchers as scissors in Beauty
Parlor, your rows of pink-bagged pumps for
Shoe Store as you patiently tried them on,
calling us all *darling*--I inherited your love
of chemistry, a reverence for life forms
both here and gone----

Ida

You went along for the honeymoon
when Flore married,
moved in and stayed on,
a Lifer, you laughed and
played Old Maid
I hated to lose that game-you
said you preferred it.

Your "mantlepiece" bodices were impressive,
your green and red shoes colored your walk at Wing's
where we could buy anything!-on Saturday afternoons
you made your only recipes, egg-toast and jello,
for nieces who hid in closets, tried to fool you
but never could as you brought us out
spinning tales of spiritualists and trips, playing
Mitch Miller favorites on your upright piano-
You left your parents' turn-of-the-century
variety near Weld Square to travel, and I keep
your cards, teacups, souvenirs from every state-
I am a virtual wanderer daily approaching millennium
but I hope to shake a leg soon
like Ida with the smiling eyes.

Albert

with your usual courtesy you gave us plenty of time
to expect your going--you were a creature of habit,
I'm fine your calling card; you fought quietly,
filtering intelligence for country and family,
messages as postmaster for the North End--our
Friday night crosswords were cryptic
tough-but I learned that listening is much
of the battle--you knew that there was a word
for everything and, if not, a silence.

today they've chosen your traveling suit
soft beige as skin, and a casket cloistered
as a confessional--private as you were,
you would like it--but I hear you choosing:

I'd rather have Louis' rides to Giammalvo's
for the Sunday roast, and even Jean's cigars,
smelling to high heaven still with us here on earth.

Alma

In Spanish alma means soul
In the Sweden you left young
it was a given name of girls--
you came to Brockton, Ma
married a man you met in the mill
where you lost fingers to a machine, served
him children and supper
while you ate after them, alone-
He said "your only friends are your family and your pocketbook"
You hired out for housekeeping
and came to us, carrying snow pudding
your own rags and advice over the kitchen sink-your
strong shoulders bore me, my heavy-headed
youth-I picked up your upswing accent and denied
Catholic heaven when it wouldn't allow you in--you were
a tall woman and grandchildren line up along your bier
mourning in front of the red curtain as I recall: "'men,
the work of the house is love"......

Bébé Soeur

Renée   you and I   are shooting rapids, tending wounds, testing
ourselves--we aren't pirates with cardboard swords,
three-cornered hats made from comics and classifieds:
    For Sale and *Lil' Abner* cavorting-- we had those Sunday rituals
all year: bowls of popcorn and Parcheesi, shaving with butter
knives and Noxema, executing death in oily Mason jars
    for the enemies of our roses, rabbits nervous they'd be next;
recall how we were divided, in seersucker, in jeans
And how now our moves defy our bolder dreams:
        Let sky-wings ring a fusillade
                To all silent   frail   blades

Epiphanies for My Father

He prepared the field well for the yield
in the tradition of his cultivator
ancestor--he produced educated
natives, marketable competitors
ready for the city. He bartered
business for reputation, lugging
sacks of paper through his father's
school past the homeside door
behind which his mother, Claudia,
cooked spaghetti suppers for the nine
plates Louis, the eldest son, had laid out.

In this waterfront town he peddled knowledge
the way hawkers do fish, personal.
sprouting through junior high, the technical
school, the university he grew through seasons
of accounts--he moved students through the courses
on a swamp-laid campus with medieval valor: the night
enveloped the tip of the campanile before his files ever
closed.   "L.J.R." harvested a New Bedford of nurses, opera
lovers, fans who waited for the curtain to part,
for the play to start.   Louie programmed English
as a second language for new émigrés, kept honest
records and Sundays, was not the Mafia accountant
and bought his meat from the good-willed Italians
at the bottom of the hill. Humble beneath his perennial
cap and shadow-French curls, his camera eye caught daughters
in parochial-checked suits and seersucker running towards
the lens, willing, eager, laughing,
growing up in the lion's eye. We are survivors
of the stone goddess with praying hands who overlooks
other women blocks from home slain, scrolled in memory
only by coroner or chief of detectives.   Papa Louis,
nothing could claim his devotion from this hotbed,
bargaining our fate between day and evening school,
sessions of piano-tennis-language lessons "save your
soul", "control your emotions", "Do it!"

At eight I stool-stepped, did inventory of New Bedford Tech
pencils and pink gummys--today I lead in precisely witness
to the silences. Whenever I open the window
inside,
I remember the shore-sandwich afternoons
when we reeled in imaginary fish with our exotic
lures. Wherever I trudge homeward, school-sack
swinging with self-creations, I think of you handsome
waving warm and gentle good-bye.
However I catch a shooting star, naturally splendid
lasting never long enough
I follow your path
with your gaze on the far star
and earth-work abundant--How there are no
words left but a caress
enveloping us all....I remember you,
Louis Papa......

the gift

My mother began to see the future when her eyesight failed her-
She went inside behind the horny cornea and saw the thorny crown
of Jesus the Christ on the image forming in the clouds.

How often she practices her prayers, her figure clasped
as a missal sealing the articulation of essence.
The marble Virgin in the yard watches, her hands touching
like wings. The angels on each side are named after daughters,
offer baskets of flowers.

Her rosary beads smell like roses in Spring.
Her recliner is damp and hot, the impress of her neckline
wreaths the toweling.
She cries sweeter tears in the house she was born in,
the rambling home mistaken for a funeral parlor.
Today the blinds are drawn and small prismatic
arcs swim in litanies of vision over the ceiling.

She takes up her needle and knits flawless designs
of the Tree of Life, remembering the celestial mafia of old:
the Jewish butcher with bloodstains on the apron,
the Italian greengrocers virile with sons, the French
priest with his square hat and home visits.

Her father was the doctor who frequented the chemistry
of fallen bodies and her boxes of canned foods are emissaries
in the tradition of this immigrant town.
The missionary tipi, erect on her t.v.,
is testament to the hearth of a woman of Mount Pleasant,
looking out over tenements shocking
blue and green of Weld Square.
She sweats, loses ten pounds, and dreams of a risen Lord.

Birthing

for Elise Marie and Gemma Claire

out of our flesh
I wove
over bone
new living
all new
born to the slap of fine strong hands
born to the pull of firm easy feet
dancing on dark water
hot belly
talking to me
soon will whet me
and a thousand seas rush meet
coagulate
in blood--issue
a deep dark vessel
sails
out from its native place
...we've gotta be
a little cocky
mama, she has the expectation
and their papa he got a lot
of soft talk to pass on.....

the love of the fish   for Thomas

We offer each other
the love of the fish
gracefully slipping through mud
believing each breath carrying
the clay, this cosmos--
the colors and shadows gently share
our air, the light is drawn to us
casting our lives in fluid fire
releasing boundaries
we float above flares in our seas
of silence, listening
for the ribbon of blues
the beauty wail
the dance of life...

Reunion

I wanted to tell you while the wind still fluttered
like an infant's eyes at first light through the Parc des Braves

I wanted to tell you as tulips nodded to the end of Quebec chill
and the sky overhead confirmed the ice had melted

I wanted to tell you all along my solitary tour of the Plains
of Abraham as I shaped images of ancestors into the clouds

I wanted to tell you when I circled your apartment building
like a cycling bird practicing to nest

I wanted to tell you as I buzzed myself into the long walk down
the quiet white corridor on tapping heels

We have found each other   you said looking up at me, and
What kind of foolishness did you do? when I gave you
a dozen roses

I wanted to tell you as you picked ferns falling from the bouquet
to your rug, glancing at my card thanking you for the greatest gift

I wanted to tell you as I tapped back down the hall to throw the
box down the chute as you requested

I wanted to tell you when you showed me my chin, my cheeks,
my smile in the photos of Fortuna and Roseanne on the back
of their holy funeral cards that Memorial Day weekend.

I wanted to tell you as I ate the instant cream of celery soup you
made for me, unknowing that it was la fête des mères in town

I wanted to tell you as I drove back to my hotel, calling as
you requested to ensure I had arrived safely
I told you and want to tell you still for the lifetime those brief moments
can never fill....

sculpting life...

the standing buddha:
raised hand of the fearless
the extended hand of charity!

the buddha in her room
has a hole in his foot,
cracked like the outlook of sorrow;
the buddha over his bed wears sunglasses
watches his mattress, leering...

the buddha under our gingko
minds the spirits of our children
oversees the garden, our family
tree

the variety of buddhas on display
in the museum distracts me--
I love the young girl whose skirt
is a hoop of carnelian flowers

the simplicity of things
we own as ours:
a box of kimono silks
a cache of writing tools
or this domestic scene:
pouch turnip pipe

south central address

I put on my trench coat and walk from the center
carrying a sack of alphabet soup-size letters
the children get when they spell correctly
the words they'll swap with the family at supper

I see ahead what I expect:
six steps up, three flights and
a staccato key, giving onto green
linoleum, half-filled
coffeecups and bony, clammy legs
thawing on the counter in the pantry--
I know you'll come in, stoop to take off your boots
shoulders slumped from what you've transported all day,
smelling of what you hold close--cod, oil, sweat--
you'll strip down and I'll run next door to throw those blues
away into the neighbor's washer for the hundredth day

we'll celebrate with chicken and laughs
you'll promise we won't live on eggs and iced tea
until spring and after dinner
we'll walk past unpainted houses, old creole homes
boarded like battened hatches-somebody's place, you'll point
with your boxer's hands and battles,
needing only a place to hang your leather,
but I think of being devoured
like animals without respect, piece meal,
always more than they take us for-
together we'll swat at air between us
static with gnats and fertilizer
we'll run with all we're worth
back to the estate where we burrow in by 10
because candlelight can't keep us warm
to make what we still can create the fair exchange: taste
                                    to touch   to taste

Syncopating Night

for the young jazzmen jammin' every Thursday

down the street to the Vets
the three friends listen to sidewalks
jazzing them with conversations-
enter the club where alternating
rhythms converse in languages
which only forgiving ears can hear
threaded through humid summer nights--
Pierre rides the slow train into this music, snapping
his Paris attention, Claudia finger popping,
Tommy soft and still watching under roof of his new fade
with hard lemonade--Art blows, Lonnie knows
his organ, and the boys brass out to the max
doing each their own ensemble
variation on the immutable scat of freedom
getting down on the weak beat
playing their dues to the night-
boogie enthralling them with its long-secret
power syncopating
yin with yang,
the boy with the man

P'town Postcard

Our young guest exchanges
as he learns English from me
"I see you have much racism here
in America, more than we do--I thought
this was supposed to be the new world?"

We talk about old money and look
all over town it's about clique over coin
as colors hang with their own until
the line where the poor split into separate quarters
west end/south end , and the rich retire
to the high end

We take him to the tip of our earth
the point of the Cape softened by dune
bumping and grinding waves on the jet-ski
is living it up--the trip into town
is the eyeful all the way alive,
as is, as live and let live,
au naturel and variations
on the chordal key
that taps the spine
and shakes heads—

"drag queens in the street, this is a gay town"
he assesses the scene from the eyes of fifteen
and Paris where quiet-as-it's-kept goes down here
artists elbow through Commercial Street
children share taffy and transvestites hang out,
parading, finding the right boutique attire:
shades shorts sandals chapeaux

tourists from Iowa waltz around campers
from Quebec, cars with New York plates defer
to pedestrians, and everybody is freer
to be—

          "I like to live it up",
gnawing prawns in an outdoor cafe
watching the stream of life
weave past his table
where the sisterly waitress
informs him "you can't drink even a sip
of French wine in America tonight!"

Island Woman's Latenight

I saw my future husband dancing
waving four arms and on them
               serpents
               womens
               horns
               evil eye charms
like holy St. Francis
fanatic burning spent
melting in the wheels of life
while even in frenzied whirls
the logic binds

I sleep with the conjur' man
who can turn the bones to rattlin'
and move them around the floor advising
no shame no blame no debt no sweat
throw yr bone into it
       and small greens-to taste!
you'll know by the way yr house smells
       when it's done
       when it's ready
       when it's done

I say to him
already
I got a dancer in my blood
I got salt in my blood
I got a queen's face in the cards
       I got lightning in my brain
       I got a hunger in my veins
for my soul
       for my soul
              for my soul

Smuggler's Den

"keep your seat and hold your hat"
says the sign on the wall-
it ain't bad advice
but nobody can do just that
as the jazz snakes through
seductive, elevating
legs, spirits, voices-
John skates the ivory board
and the company's cookin'
in a cavern of sound--
coleus, peaceful flight,
names for bands organic like
rain, like dancing on mist
up and down your spine-
Bobby Greene blows mean
and Armstead is smooth as his tux
baby, you got your groove

the Elks, the Main Event:
nod and bow deep to those nights
twisting into drive, turning
a winking eye in your direction-but
Smuggler's was the joint
where you could barbecue your meat
in a fireplace rubbing elbows with a stranger
on a sofa like an old
friend,
that was the day
in New Bedford
at Billy Woods on the wharf
all gyratin', me with a wallbanger in one hand
and a pen on the table, reviewing
                    the scene to turn ya'll on

Song of the Sea Gypsy

In a town of mean proportion
In a time of high degree
lived a man with loose and fast ways
they called the Sea Gypsy

He toured the island people
In his Buick like a ship
with a phone in every project
and a flask above the hip--
He dealt the cards as Dr. Love
at the bank of heart's desire
and he played you close
and he played you out
as he set himself on fire-

He swallowed Southern Comfort
and ate the Cuban cooking
hot and liquid on the tongue
like nightlife he was hooking--
the drums they beat his song out
his heart was like a drum
it kept the beat of blood alive
              as the fierce spirits hummed

The men looked to him for their deals
the women craved his kiss
his partners mutinied themselves
he toughed out what they missed

He traveled storefront cafes,
sometimes Rico's, some days Phil's
but his favorite place was Niki's
where the hostess foots the bill
              she runs her little parlor
like a ramblin' roadhouse show
you never knew just how you'd leave
this lady's gamblin' row

Some say he was a loner,
say wolf, say killer shark
but there breathes another woman
whose lips say he held hearts

Latin cooking, Latin heels
stepped out through his dreams
he tracked their lively sound down
to the arms of a voodoo queen--
He put away his potions
to try her herbs and roots
she traded lonely nights away
for a life of love and loot

They glowed, the place grew brighter
as 'round the block the story goes
say, a man found the Ecstasy Candle
that was lit one night long ago--
Then they jailed the voodoo princess
for having an eye so sly
and a hand that that slipped in pockets
                and stirred up skin every time

Since then the man with flint-like eyes
struts in the pool hall all day
hustling action before he dies
his dues way past paid
he sees life from the wings of a stick
the angles are judged and timed
he plays with the grace of that creole queen
                and the memory of natural highs
His soul dreams of the tropics
His Indian blood's his case
that pride and power shining
history etched upon his face
You can catch him some days in the mirror
going through changes again-
his touch and taste so familiar
                you know, now, he's going to win!

Spring Poem—Renewal at the Immigration Rally, April 10, 2006

Hermanas,
we welcome you
into this month of the Fish moon,
Egg moon: when Sky is full of itself
  Sprouting grass running the ground

Well of course, could we do any different...
We live in the city of fish
Number one fishing port in Americanation
Your tribe scaling, gutting in its grey Atlantic
the way we don't want to need to do.

We welcome you hermanos
not quite like the woman who hands out sweatshirts ID-ing
as "Americans too" your eddy of baseball-
capped workers, hundreds representing still more   low-profile,
triangulating the space between our institutions,
City Hall and the Free Public Library,

implicated in an America
you cannot read,
faces open as sunflowers
chanting litanies of "si se puede"—"it can be done" possible at last
all you could ever do

unlike the missionary who thinks you should have stayed in Mexico,
unlike the Mayor's call

for ID cards and above-the-table deals
with your consulate and our government
watching,
most unlike the suit with a gun in one pocket
and a flask in the other
grinding your generations to their knees
unlike the tall men, the CEO's who can never meet
your eyes,
unlike the thinkers expressionless under their shades

     A native drum remembers you
Compadres
Your eager faces, the tiny flags wafting the April breeze
waved by brown arms of children who
 no doubt
will be taller than you thanks to price rite
and the free health
center
It beats wel/come
Be a-
ware
in this cost-effective
corp-o-nation built on a free
labor pool

     Y cuando diga *Libertad*

Me dicen *Muere*!*   (twice, louder the 2nd time)

Echoes of homeland

We,

The children of immigrants, slaves, Native

human beings welcome you....stand with you

waxing toward fullness, Egg moon expands through dying light,

benevolent in its moment of Unity,

our humpbacked flute player, your Aztec song.

* when I say *Freedom*, they tell me *'die'*

Otto René Castillo, Guatemalan poet and revolutionary, murdered by the junta in 1968

Update:

A federal raid, managed by Immigration and Customs Enforcement agents supported by local police and sheriff backup, rounded up 375 undocumented factory workers at Michael Bianco, Inc., in New Bedford, MA on March 6, 2007. They were detained in Massachusetts or Texas and ultimately deported. Many left families behind with little or no means of support. Most had been working for years producing gear for the U.S. military and contributing to life in the City.

A brief history of New Bedford, Mass.

A child's clock, calendar, compass

We started watching for the waffle man
for his white wagon
in June, he came once a year
with those waffles sprinkled with sugar
or plain, in August

There was no radio or t.v.
When an event happened, day or night,
Elections or fires,
Extras were issued:
  "Extra, extra....read all about it!"

          "Any rags, any bottles, any bones today"
the ragman cried. He was an old Jew:
"If you don't keep quiet, he'll take you along",
          memère whistled between her teeth,
a handy threat companion to the clop-clack-clop
of his buckboard on the cobblestones
 once a week, sometimes twice
at any time.

The milkman came by everyday
at a reg'lar time, 3 or 4 on Mount Pleasant-
Dion's had wagons white as milk,
 White's had the red and white ones!

It cost 10 cents a quart.
Mr. Tracy drove the ice by twice
each week at the time memère was braiding my hair
for school--
It cost a penny a pound.

Every Friday was Fourth of July!
The Fish man would come by
blowing his horn,
He kept the fish undercover
on ice behind two little doors in back of his buckboard.
"Fish" he'd call out in thick Yiddish.

About 1880-1890
When great-grandma and grandpa came from Connecticut
the center of New Bedford was between Weld Square
and Linden Street.
Officer Kelly's beat was Weld Street. We made up a song about him:
            "Old Mr. Kelly had a pimple on his belly,
                his wife took it off, and it tasted like jelly"

Michel Mathieu had a *pinceare*, a Van Dyke...
Aunt Ally washed it clean from his tobacco juice!
Uncle Pit, or Pierre, was born normal
until kids playing on the 4th of July threw him in a well.
He got lung inflammation, complications-he became
a hunchback, had a big moustache,
Really *bent*, but laughing eyes,
drank a little-friendly with Mayor Ashley-

Got a job as a street cleaner: his wagon was a garbage can with
wheels—

His wife was a hypochondriac who ate only stuffed pigeon as meat-

They lived on Holly Street

He made excellent chop suey in the pantry, we called it *botterie*

in those days, his daughter married a Sevigny.

There was no North End, South End.

Trolley cars ran on Purchase up Union

Through Park, Sixth Street up to Elm

to Summer and Cedar.

There was a trolley to Fall River,

one along the Fairhaven Bridge,

another along Main Street in Fairhaven

to Fort Phoenix.

Mr. William B. Dooley ran the New Bedford-Fall River run.

They ran on Acushnet Ave. to Tarklin Hill

and on North Front, joining at the junction

at Bailey's Square.

The number 276 ran down South Water Street

where the Cape Verdeans set up homes and

boarding houses and the Jews had their stores.

Granma Claudia's father put his barbershop

pole down there on Rivet Street.

Some trolleys had no sides, were open

with long seats and straps to hang onto.

They were scrapped for the war effort.

When we took the trolley downtown

for a soda at Woolworth's

or a visit to Wings,
We would head to Union Street
near the Institution of Savings
to see the Italian with his high-crowned,
feathered hat and hurdy-gurdy--
He placed a little seat in the gutter
for his monkey.
After the tune had been played, he released
the leash. The monkey tipped his red cap
for money. He emptied it into a green velvet
drawstring bag. He would make his rounds
and remember who gave—he was smart, that little beggar!

The umbrella man was an old Italian, too,
with his cart made up like a roll-top desk with tools inside-
There were two huge wheels to roll on, and
a flint wheel on one side, a cup and pail for water
to make it go on the other--
He repaired the umbrellas and knives, sharpened knife and scissors.
We heard his song once a week at any time:
                    "Umbrellas to mend"

We watched for the coal man
in the winter
His two horses, his wagon with a chute
sticking way out in back to dump
chestnut coal and pea
the small ones   lost in our fists

Steam

What it took to transform S/V Ernestina

He was ignited, breathing
the revolution on the waterfront
one day at a time
biking t-shirted, humping the cobblestones
wind whipping between the handlebars
smacking him in the face,
embarking at Coal Pocket Pier
like a new maridu
greeting his love, climbing over the side,
hands made to shoot hoops
wide open

Below decks, he wrenched gut
Transformed bits of shard, ancient
Cod-bone   peeling his skin,
Sinew   sweat
        Shape:
        The ribs, how will She run
back
to Djabraba
shore   set   free
so sabi song
in the sail of a new millennium—

The replicas of slave ships

ease their karma knowing She exists
as they make the best of history,
job market, working that theater of the absurd
to reclaim those terrible hollers
into the mantle of *mar,*
Pirating booty in the biographies
of the Black men who grind,
Salt, and steam into being
the struts of *this* stage,
churning waters into motion,
the grist of who we were
Meant to be......

maridu—husband
Djabraba-island of Brava
sabi—nice, happy
mar-sea

Hale Ma`o Makani (Home of Green Wind)

Bridge to ohana
Portal to the womb of time
Ma`o makani

Out from Hanalei

The Coconut Man in his grass skirt
chops cubes of white delight
from the back of his truck
for Bali Hai beachers
trying to stay wet
at the end of the passable
Rainbow'd Road

Naming the Wind

Wind whips like rain
through the Traveller's Palms,
the jacaranda bobbing a violet dance
to the house of the sun,
Kai ke`oke`o,
    nightlong white sea song
insisting that
Rooster awaken

In our bed of broken leaves
We entwine our dreams
Lovers   Sidesteps
Confirming
Our sacred lava dance of Life
In this circle of flowers
Salt
And seaspray
   Taste and be forever
Broken away
Floating on the island
Of the holy do-ing
Belling the air
Stirring it up....

the muse in blazes

woman of mysteries
woman of desire
                I have burned a thousand faces
                into my heart, cut with an incisive knife
                words for kindling

storming the woods
on an uneven path
I fan the flames of desire,
violins serenade the search
galloping horses prod the butter moon as
she dangles the white snake suspicion
but we are born in the flanks of wolves

baptized by cloaked familiars
we lay our heads on books of fable
we meet on common ground
under the burgeoning crescent, the deep
recess of moon

the horizon is cut to a puzzle
the pieces threaten descent
clouds are restless
as a covey in the mackerel sky
                I remember how marimba mapped the spine
                the bass hugs the walls of the body
                we are piped to piercing clarity
                magnificent as our mask falls,
revealing
legs as gates of pearl
thighs lush as thyme
the angel spreads soft wing
in the space behind the knee
in the palm the swallow solos

breasts hum in the kaballah light
neck sinewy strong, mouth

a fortress tempting the tidal sea,
burst smile is a run through poppies
golden throat weaves a basket around the sun,
encapsules the mistral wind
my voice will play out the harmonies of the heart
moved by the tongue that has no root
        the tongue that sprouts wings and flies
        the tongue past all naming
        the tongue of saying
        the tongue the mother shares
        the tongue that the soul sings
        the tongue that sings the soul

I want to burn my flagrant mouth
on the pinion of a dove
I desire with a blueblack heart
the hummingbird who stole from the shawl
of day

This passion overrides
the gape of the grave
the space before silence--
curls back
after lashing us
to expectation
love pyre is
phoenix fire
defying death, extinguished
on flesh

As dawn over the eastern wall, welcome!
I bury my smoldering dreams
I ignite myself on the vein inside
your thigh, in the small of your back
I rise from your side,
how morning turns the tide,

we have eaten the heart of the lioness
we carry in our back pocket the eagle of Russia

in our basket of eggs the pyramid-bomb

I hope on hibiscus
the hem of a gardenia
I have etched your face behind my eyes
and carry your paisley flight
in the ebony of my lifeline
              we arise! aroused flush
with blue dawn
cupped whole by the spirit, I
shorn by your eyes,
           the muse in blazes

Note: I broke free decades ago from the mindset of those male
poets who referred to me as a muse, specifically their muse,
while refusing to acknowledge my work as equal to their task.
As I grew stronger in my voice as a woman, as a poet, and
as a feminist, I realized the muse within me fostering my work.
It is this anima that animates the poem which, when viewed in this
light, is not "surreal" but rather real exploration of the poet's
psyche rising above the glass ceiling.
Jung's theory of anima as "the woman within" the male artist
can be applied to the woman within the female artist waiting to
be birthed into consciousness. If we love her, we will give her
voice—so this is a love poem, after all.

Overtime

through great gaping sobs into sheets
i called out a name no one owns
imagining
        ten toes, ten fingers
to curl around mine
they'd be hanging like a monkey from a bar
or clutching like a guerilla with a loaded gun

this is a dangerous operation
opening
this is a conspiracy between the throbbing thighs
and the white screen of mind as sheet of memory:
I uncovered the male in my youth, reading
through the night under a percale tent
with a small light and a book of words.
Later, ravaged, tonight I remember lighting
the last match in a damp, dark closet:

you smell the sulfur first,
touch the cool lead bullet
with your foot, and the fur it freezes--
a live creature is grooming his coat and cleaning his teeth
in the corner, waiting to discover you
grazing a gaze on your fat toes--
your neck bristles, your breasts report
like any explosive
and you leap, the retort
flushing the dark chamber--
what chemistry confronts your face,
your singed hair
and jumps out at you
        with another dimension

The Birth of a Poet

In the space between heartbeat and breath
In the silence between revelry and dream
I swam sinuous
through hoops of love,
rings of fire...how
that snake, suspicion, coiled
in circles of desire—

expanding my stone weight and resolve,
I resonate to walls
chimes crystals
revving the velocity
and ventriloquist that is god
to pure pitch

THE VISIBLE THE ESSENTIAL THE OTHER

our swift and devouring meat,
the sinew of paw
to calf, the mooncalf
that is madmoon seer spiritual
subverting the tyger's sheathed
and subtle turns--I bounced
into this sphere between forceps and forced
faith, a witness to
the shapes we share:

a trinity of rings
wedding this form, I be
the apparent,
the transparent,
                    the other!

A Walk in the Woods

This bridge is a body
your kisses explode above it
like stars
       the knit of lovers
a whirlpool of diamonds

kachina has bedded
the bank
with seed
clean sheets of fiddleheads—
   surrender the thorny bridle of sex.

That changeling, fear
is the path of zen
the shuffling of poets
exposing themselves
with lucid genuflection--
   the cradle of our world
   the phoenix in the sun

The music in your voice
makes this readable,
sounds the now,
the bell of breakfast
the tense of bacon and eggs
buddha-belly asks ponderous questions
            ahead of us, goat-man
            transcribes--the index of experience
            you, tantric dove, codex of innocence

In a cathedral of trees
the shrine is small
as womb
as the arch of two knees

Sailing to Santorini

Under a cliffed sky
outreaching
the fort rings in
ripples
fraying out evenly
to that stray of beached desires,
the shell of Dilos

Here
in the star-hulled caique
we have christened the waters
outmaneuvered the sun
dazzling the lions of Apollo
with our brilliance
retrieving Kalypso for our mother
we bury the tidal rage

In this crescent stretch
we baked our dreams
with the leaven of lava
in the kiln of unplumbed water
pressing the almond eyes of the poppy-
seed-girl between the hillocks
of powder

      we are wash home, Thira
to scale your face
charting on the grace of Emborion
we will dance our thanks
in the shelter ray
of your far-flung
laughing fire--
praise for vessels: the sturdy navel
and the full belly

house of leather, house of grass

torrential waters flow over the rim
of a kiosk in the tropical midday
and the highest power holds the reins
of some far star, directing
my marionette dance to the cosmos
jerky and panamerican on this planet

living in the hotbed, tuned in tandem to revolution
i anticipate constantly the wrench of geographies,
land masses tossed like elbows, knees, boots
into the cauldron of millennial fire igniting
like delicate grasses
activated by stars shooting insolent in their splendor

I read the covey of birds fanning the rainforest sky
the constellations poised like a clutch of arrows
against a blueblack altar cloth--
pulled into the suck of our sacrificing days
we move to these stations like pilgrims
guided, lighting small candles to the far star--
the deluge on earth star pours Spirit over All
communion falls like light
wordless, breathable, surging to sound
like wind on wing

exercise for flesh and blood

"you want me..
to lay back?" she gulps
gut tilted in the dentist's chair,
face red with the spotting of expectant
middle-age scanning the ceiling for cracks,
crack, break your mother's...she feels the gas, the warmth
of even breathing, his stomach rises and falls
like a slow bellows near her cheek, the bubble
contracts around his smile as he manipulates
the bones of her head, rearranging the beautiful
death of the woman she was-- each cell in this new

atomic woman sings, the small jaw unfolds
like the mouth of a fish unraveling from the hook
of time in the evolution of some higher
species--
her reclining moments progress like cusp of moon or tooth,
chewing each second that radiates pain on the red vector--
waves on a screen vibrate life's delirious beat
as he chips on creating a new arsenal of weapons.

Spine straight, she rises sliced and stitched and
shifted by the stream of surgery which compels:
the memory of fantasies that ricochet
back with the velocity of a marooned lover
rescued by a stranger, the articulation
of she who cast off a ragged rap, feeding now
silently on the miracle between the hungry miles
and the mirror framing for the instant
the level rows of bones in a universal smile.

Sleeping In

When a woman wishes
she owned the beautiful face
of a clock with hands like water
she points the arrow of the mood
wheel on her wall toward the blue vector
and goes from bed to bed in brocade
attic rooms hung with black crows
dreaming through the windows of a man in smoke-filled dens
whose eyes let the ocean in

the louvered house he owns crowns the county of men in black
slacks, black slickers, banking fires
that execute the leaves even in burning rain
the wives wear aprons with small faces
on them, hair burnishing the back of their knees
as they move cool around each acre

this man in velour rolls a tired eye
to the ceiling, envisioning the advent
of his brood mare of good stock
clumping to the terrace off his library
written by those who assumed voices
and names—
this woman dreaming makes out the book
with short tropes and image of a fighting cock on the cover
as her own--she tosses to the sound of squirrels in the wall
clambering to break out--her skin breathes sweat
as she wakes, picks up her side with hand heavy as paw

she unwinds thinking of torrid climes, the bride price--
when she follows the banister down to supper she checks for first
snow through the peephole-- she finds a changed status, a convex
clapboard street that distances each close passing car, relaxes
the steep hill ahead of her into one long, plain road

Suite for Planet X

For Raumjard

the Key to the Infinite

Beauty--some say
open up the left palm--
my velvet pouch is ready
heavy with lies
hangs above my bed swinging
the oils for my body
I am suspicious of the very sleeve
of experience, even though I've wiped
big beefy tears on it
fractured them into 1,000 crystals
illusions as mirrors
fall
into the mana, the music!

the Emperor has no Clothes

Truth--some say
piercing the earth
with bright sun-arrows
to bow to beauty--
ravishing us with the innocence
of a humble schoolgirl
winking behind the skirts of a promiscuous nun

the human touch
when there is still room left in the fantasy
for a finger, for dramas played out
on bodies whose contours don't matter--
all comparisons are odious,
small flags at half-mast to an ideal
that is not the ladder of heaven,
that ladder swings with you--

Inward

they have power for what they are:
words, tools, body
        image
piecing a montage of self-dictation
everything is a clue to the cartographers
but whose mythology is your metaphysic?
there is one map
there is one voice
to speak the demography of the soul:
Yours!
what is real:
the shape of the world
the words are filler--Fool!
what is hidden/what you see is
the alphaomega of its own questioning
Lies exist on myriad levels but
we often get those we expect
to each according to his need

Beyond

some monks climb mountains
seeking the highest point
they want to stop dreaming
some settle in the dunes
blow their voices to god
not so? the body reveals
revels
records everything
weight of breath
is the essence of art
in flesh I expand to you

struggling for the word--eat it, feed it--
the writing of it
and the experience of it
are the same

there is no question
only in the corner of our eye
someone who catches
and gives the image sight
in our attempts to make the circle
of love, in our creation of ways
to confirm our many tears
we lay out our props
on the table calling it
life's Banquet
whirling
with poetry's magic skirt
breath into being

Proof of love: you can't ask for it
but here it is--
      even the long distance runner loves
      the glutted along with the gourmet
      Gauguin dolorosa
      the painted dragon
      tiny fireflies freed to love
  all trampoline through the deep, the fog
  the blanket of infinity
   shadowing light--it's a family fetish.

Hegira   ...events of April , 1997

"My work requires infinite eggs to come to birth
      in Eternity" says Old Allen,
not copping out,
hatching all along the waysides of tears.
Smiling under his soul-saucer eyes,
tired of loving but Joy surpasses it
like a moon hung upside down,
mouthing it off fervor and flame,
he gassed it up nights bygone,
padding down gently the rooms
of his mind, the white spaces
empty with Naomi, Ti-Jean, his throbbing
head, a global squeezebox,
brimming over his green light

The Maynards he converted,
the flannel greys--fruity tartness
all over yr screen--tongue
vibrating rolling his lines
dripping with vials of glory gone down
--now Allen dead, not alien
to the world, hatching
the revolution in his pink cardigan,
tossing shellbits o' poem from pockets,
tending the vines on his rooftop garden,
watering us daily with shaloms
sung fainter, cracking our global air...

here, I listen   make   do
having lost artifacts of dream,
numerous airtight embryos,
balloon egos of dilettantes popping 'til dawn,
the manse of family I'd taken on
until I was taken out of the bourgeois fold,
gone like the lovestabs that giving gets--
left with media filters of guns and drugs,
insurrections on NPR and the circus

of highway circuits, networks, "news"
of house burnings, flammable dollars
laid as wallpaper in the White-Dream-FunHouse

I moved with Allen, in millennium, mutinied matter
object-less, looking for turf, for community
in old North End New Bedford Franco house
blocks from "Doc's" office across from St. Antoine' s (back
in the day)
I am small again by instances, by images of millworker émigrés on
wall, plying paper, rope, hair--ephemera into art of nest--writing
by warmth of dragon-grin space heater,
energy food and herbals in sky-high cupboards--
I call again on Spirits, the grove of ancestors: I'd patted
the ground over their heads, kneeling on Kebec green
square acre of Ancienne Lorette--

the lord is shepherd under hawk's wing
gliding above the ghosts of longhouses,
village, grandfather, pepère
gave good medicine
charmed the serpent onto his stone
marker   Docteur Belleau
he buried the dead
shoeless so they will
dance with the stars

moi, aussi, healing and healed
willing to bow to NoThing
but my own beard brilliantly alive
survived...Freewing and Hatching....
("Money against Eternity" says Allen
lest we forget)

Culebra

your hills rise from the bay,
breasts of sisters
stretched in sun-
splendid
necklace
of light from punta soldado
to mosquito bay,
nursing a hundred
visions, ghosting a thousand
dreams the
black volcanic
past lurks beneath
coral bones, pipes, spirals
spewed on beach and bleached
with tropical insistence:
the value of heat,
the resonance of shell
on air
mid-ear.

gringos trudge through town
local folk swap tales and pedal
swirling the days
between their feet,
coasting over slopes
greeting scarlet coxcombs,
kittens and kids
diving
off ferry docks to show off
for mainlanders from Fajardo
over for the weekend barbecue

la playa fills with campers dancing
to salsa on memorial day
weekend in this u.s. territory
the ragged perros run
to tables hunting scraps,

isla nena air hums and slices the horizon
with suspended hope of small pleasures—
currency of coconut, karma
in the journey—

we have ferried here
with cargo of cars and sweating
straw-brimmed faces
los ricos anchor their yachts and
feast at mamacita's--we eat street
food, jumbo shrimp and chicken
served by brown boy-cousins
seducing walkers on a spice-
scented path to their snorkel
for dorado-

Culebra, which transformation
will your heat and light spark....
which body pass through the mirror
of sea and rise from the dive
with fistfuls of gold, sand
as the looking glass
of our Caribbean smile.

whiskey tango kilo

for Schooner Ernestina, homeport New Bedford, MA, and
those who love her

The body of this poem, beginning after the music fades, can be
delivered by a single poet or more than one voice. Since the poem
was written to capture the spirit of many who contributed to the
vessel's transformation, alternating voices at appropriate beats
would help fuse content and performance form.

First Voice (Creole rhythm): Ernestina, SV/CV
Second Voice (American rhythm): WTK, over
Pause--no response--
Second Voice: WTK, WTK...whiskey, tango, kilo, over
Echoing Voice (from audience): Copy that!
First Voice: Copy that.

Music (begin with Cape Verdean tunes and segue to sea songs)

Poet:
> whiskey tango kilo
> that sparks images: raising rigging, first in 1894
> raising lines to Liberty Sail 1986
> blowing wooden flute aloft to the moonraker,
> raising flags: African corn, solidarity stars

Event-full:
> sleek Grand Banks hull cod fisher Morrissey designed-
> Bob Bartlett peers into sextant to the Pole 600 miles away-
> Cap'n Dan over Bartlett's marker in Newfie Park-
> They bow, do history, keeping their heads from 65 feet
> of Boom

They meet in the triangle of time:
Morrissey to give her speed
landing cod in 1912 record runs--
Bartlett exploring Arctic
blowing up ice to get through,

surveying for Smithsonian specimen
hunts from '26 near twenty years...he's done, She's
retired, transformed by fire—
salvaged by Henrique Mendes
a packet for free people coming to America..
chicken and children between the isles...

dismasted en route to '76 bicentennial
She veers to Africa, is overhauled-
In '82 Norm Gomes brings Her back
a gift between nations-
Tom Lopes fights to legislate Her home
in Mass., Joli Gonsalves
commissions Her beauty
in festival, John Bullard throws his
WHALE behind Her-

New York harbor OP Sail to Liberty '86,
South Street Seaport, we made it!
from bluefish and blue dawn over Padanaram Harbor...
Tommy Grace with bandaged hand thick as a fist
from laying ballast to get Her there,
Joey Gelband spidering the lines,
Nancy and Norm placing the serendipity boom
we'd found to replace our broken one
magic at the berth we'd been assigned
by mistake—

heading OP Sail
with the Eagle, fireworks
for our labor of love--black and white
together as family ne'er seen before
nor since-- it's there in the hands
          weathered and worn
          stained with the tar like Craig Walsh's sails

          it's there in the hands
          rope-lined and strong
          hauling line, polishing cowl,

heaving a beer or a song

more than a hundred spectators,
sailors, descendants on the 106
feet of deck, Capt. Dan's Swedish
teacher tours the new Cummins engine--
an international crowd applauds ....

the suits in bureaus
dismissed Cap'n. Dan
alleging him as a thief of the money
(they refused to give up any
to keep history afloat -no line item for Ernestina)
despite the fight by maverick Dan,
cabo verdes and local descendants
who'd fought for long-sought independence
of their country from Portugal
out of the Vets Hall, the 'hood

Stranded in Miami '92 when Hurricane Bob
struck the fears of inexperienced youth sail trainees,
unprepared to sail or to live in racial harmony—
rescued by Tom and Norm braving 60 foot waves
with a crew of yacht sailors out for the cruise
of their lives! New Bedford cited them all
for bravery and service to the City

DEM hired Capt. Swanzey to take the helm,
he became CEO as the state took control--yet
Her Centennial was celebrated by artists and sailors
and landlubbers, too, in Waterfront Park
                three days of music and stories
                of the struggles and quest
                and the cultures which made her
                unofficially blessed

today She floats in Boston harbor
taking on experiential learners and kids,
the elderly, disabled, and those who can afford
the safe, local lessons in the mechanics of line or life—

Capt. Dan circumnavigated the global promise,
inviting risk-takers to transform their essential selves,
sending web logs of Fiji splendor and shipboard pranks
on the Picton Castle, forcefully freed from his beloved WTK,
Ernestina...like Her, he still revels, survives....

all those who have loved Her and continue,
we'll be back, shedding our outworn roles,
for new purposes beyond the membership sail,
blowing our blues harps,
hauling our politically-wiser selves
to another turn in the destiny wheel,
raising our eyes to yet another
flag

> it's there in the hands
> rope-lined and strong
> hauling line, polishing cowl,
> heaving a beer or a song

First and Second Voices--whiskey tango kilo...do you read me?
Audience members (standing individually)--I copy that!

Note: I was inspired by my own participation as a journalist
covering OpSail '86 who opted to crew out. Much of my
inspiration in developing images comes from the wonderful
photo collage designed by Tom Grace to capture history
via the news and from images in his photographs from his own
journeys. The people mentioned herein were essential in creating
a new life for Ernestina. They were visionaries who believed and
loved before it was "politically correct" or "regionally touristic"
to do so. These are the real heroes of the story, motivated by
respect for Her in Her many incarnations and faith that they could
continue the tradition. Bless 'em all!

Update: Despite the fact that the ship has sailed under U.S., Canadian,
Cape Verdean, and Portuguese flags, she has been dockside in New
Bedford since '04, awaiting funding that will enable critical repairs.
She is a survivor through many transformations—let's get her sailing.

Butler Flats Light

We drop our mooring
in line with Butler Flats light
pulsing from its whitewashed
house in sequence after red,
then green, buoy shines shielding nightray—
the Schiamonchi ferries to Billy Woods Wharf
looming large on the horizon,
the mushroom holds fast our "joie de vivre",
twenty-two feet of dream
as the wake and waves toss us sideways
into each other—
                    Tonight
we came to untangle lines, to bail
the thunderstorm away
steps from our street,
the shingled cottage
lamps that illumine Kama's stealthy paw
in the garden or the skunk as it passes under the mystery-
bean tree on his nightly jaunt—
we've tended the earth
with hands that encircle
our love like the hedge rounding our corner,
keeping good company in, disaster out—
as we reach shore secure
smelling of brine and salt, we lift gear,
look back under the pie-slice moon
at a red-and-rocking bottom
that says our sails will unfurl
beneath another sun…

The Tree of Life

For the celebrants at the feast of Sao Pedro, Buttonwood Park, June 25, 2000*

Living, breathing
Artifacts of country:
Shiny banana blades slicing sky,
Hard, green mangos,
Sunset-red pineapple, coconut
Fish-eyed bread gazing down on me
from the triangle of boughs
reaching toward clouds
above the forty-foot mast
To Sao Pedro, patron of all islands
in the archipelago of dream-diaspora—

They gather around the wooden vat
tropical flowers over scene of *piton*
on shirts   dust still on feet
colexa, the pounding,
powdering maiz with po' sticks
sifting harvest into baskets as bassdrum
sounds conga-hot,
the dancing line weaving through the crowd
catches coin in their skirts
non-stop into the still light eve
of volleyball, strollers in American parkside
ritual

"you gotta bend, you gotta sweat"
the woman instructs survival
showing how to tip the bat-
the police stand by for a riot,
yanking cane and handing it out-
A long, brown arm reaches up,
grabs a stalk--
soon the mastro's pulley changes everything,
moving accessible wealth into our path:
Greedy boys tear chunks of sweetbread
Lovers lick cane
Sao Pedro smiles from his banner like the toddler
waving the Cape Verdean flag from father's shoulders
as he bounces to the beat of the new longitude,
the latitude of tchuba, rain, near their tree of life
like manchupa in the kettles under the tent flooding belly
like conga fueling blood

*Celebration is island-specific in Cape Verde -eg., on Brava, the
festival of S. Jodo Baptista is commemmorated on June 24th

Light on the Quequechan

for the Franco millworkers on Fall River's Quequechan River and
New Bedford's Acushnet River

waters

spinning

wheels

grind days

resourceful as bobbins

winding fast

the global investment

mamans box *graise de roti* sandwiches

ancestors eat among the congress of reeds

crows cawing

beneath blue steam

evaporate before the eyes

of we who inherit

their generous dream

light tumbles from bowl full of sky

covering Jack and Ti-Jean

distanced by degree

of latitude, *piastres*

the piano in the foyer

daughters boarding at Jesus-Marie

America, we came

For *les p'tits*

for them to swallow more
than dirt   snow slumber
under the spell of homebrew
moonshine

We tread through Flint, Globe, Highlands
on frugal stones we shape ourselves
free from debt to a past we did not earn
This light of the Quequechan
Plisse les yeux, mon vieux
at the sight of our children
swinging their lunch pails through tall Indian grass
miles to mills, the textile school:
Here spirals
The bloodred dye of our lives

Graise de rôti—aspic-like delicacy from pork roast drippings
Piastres—slang for dollars
Les p'tits—little ones
Plisse les yeux—squint your eyes
Mon vieux—old pal

In Paris

no roof is grey
coq-crimson tiles nudge dawn
into breaking
heart over early morning lace
hung on lines flapping wind
over the stone porches by graffiti-
strewn rails where women with weaves,
flocks of white-winged frocks, fly from St. Ouen
into the city to make our beds, regal-
while in the glamour quarter,
we sit scrawling postcards in Café Flore
watching the talking flirt
lean toward the slim-legged leather
Juliette, or the couple in counterpoint:
literary lenses above his beard, reading
to a lover or mentor in matronly print
punctuating the brilliance with bon-mot—

We walk the weary banks of the river
digesting our coupe glace, our rhum grogg
into millennial blood transporting
our huge appetite for wonder coursing
like our eyes on the storm-ravaged Seine rushing
so high that no boat can float under the bridges,
illuminated arches connecting pale marble gods
to these global cameras striving to remember

which angle of light best captures the look of lovers,
the round face of a newborn's awe-driven,
 natural sight

The Saint with the Shiny Foot

He inhabits his tarnished body
from a white throne in St. Germain.
We know he is a saint by the halo inclined
over his head of dark beard.
He has been the touchstone for many hands,
his right foot sparking holy memories
Conundrums and quests in the rubbing.

His benevolent gesture recalls the alms-
giving bishop, the poor crying from the jail
this abbey had been pre-Bastille--
revolution inflamed this sainted
City of marble, metal, granite gods and ghosts
with which we share our air,
the dust of those who won't crumple beneath
our compassionate touch, swept up each night

We come at it with lenses bared like teeth
shredding memory of sinewy stone
into the fiber of our art, skating
dangerously on the sculptor's pool of desire

for indestructible
Breathing

 The strut of lights in the night-street,
carousing, greets us with an imprint of Paris:
running lights on the Boulevard
seen from the Eiffel on high as the jigsaw pilgrimage,
felt here as the votive of faith
discovering our faces in the headlights
moving into our own historical encounters toward grace

Bayou Greens

> "we got a saying 'round heah:
> Gotta watch yur 3 r's:
> rodents, rats, and relatives"
> Louie Leblanc

Is ninth generation
Louisiana man in the Barataria swamps
            "my grandfather gave me everything I had
                and taught me everything I know"
passes his album with photos of family, Jesus
and gators ambling, staring
gutted and skinned like fish

            "oh *yeah*" peppers his stories
like his one-liners
            "vien ici" he invites the grown gator
who eats out of his hand like a pup
a tourist asks about shrimp
            "you push the button there, yeah…
                the Japanese have the market..
                we get 21 cents a pound now..
                when I used to tell that, I used to cry"

Lafitte hid his treasure
under the cypress,
Among the myrtle and sweet-smelling bay—
Louie
outfitted in camouflage greens
motors close so we can snatch a scent,
Confesses he often missed the school boat
from the raft pick-up station we pass—

Bayou life is learning how to survive
with the unseen
around us
like a gator in hibernation

---

who slows his heart to one beat per hour—
We pause
in awe at reptilian time
in the slow motion of our tour
through creeping vines hiding waterway homes on stilts
where tables are set with elderberry wine
For evening when truth be told
So to be
Not lost   forever

..................the other side..........

The Other Side of Where I Used to Live

there is a dog with a broken jaw
there is a man with a missing leg
there is a young girl who has turned
a loose leg
of a chair into a gun
there is a woman in parts
who can shatter tears
into crystal
there is a boy who moves only
to the kinetic pole/magnetized

I'm calling the woman Jenny
like another in my experience
who'd call out "Fire"
on the white nights in the long ward

Under the worn, distressed fabric
is the heart of the Honeymans,
father and mother beat out their moves,
he cycled from house to house
gathering junk before yard sale days, she tied
her pants with rope before it became the fashion
(she came to clean and left spider's webs--I found
in corners, admiring the maneuvers of underfoot
creatures that survive)

She came Here
to grow up
she discovered she was nobody's
daughter Here, her autograph
insufficient so she was
lingering in clinic halls
occupied with the fusion
of nerve and bone and no time
to make more of it, she walked around
with holes in her head

She believes

that as long as she bleeds she'll survive
is proud to be a woman because
"it'll come without me havin to look for it"
once a month she thinks on a man and
"wished it was as easy as hookin' a rug"
each knot a secret thrall

Her Pictures

converge and overlap in slipknots blueblack
rugs black and red, meant to be walked on
she has to call them like cards in the endless
rounds she spins through her afternoons:
"arc tree bridge"-- they are all
from the earth, outreaching skyward,
you can lose your balance and fall off"

Which of these is true? she'll test the guests
"All all --they are like a story
some woman would build, so she could
better climb, ya know it!"

Family Album

a woman and a man
there was only one way to make it
in your time
between the open valves
my mother's legs
steam heat and babies
parting
in tenements
where air is tight and hot
in a room like a closed fist
turned in upon itself
where couples claw
through the debris
of words between them
after a few
over coffee or on
the line
we reroute
                    the skeletal pasts

with our lifelines
the scrapbook patchwork
of our story:
here you are
last year with the dodge
truck-- a beauty
heavy with hiroad junk,
battered by what she does best
here you are
with alice at mickey d's
tight skirt and shimmy
               take her nowhere, like her kids

dabbling with coffee--
she sure is pretty, her husbands say
they're hard on her but

she's built for speed
nobody can make her shift
where are you now?
mama!
in some flat
with empties by the door
one tomato in the fridge
and a hot house full of children...?
a dark beard between your thighs
probing probed and never knowing
this daughter
going down before altars and beds
looking for deliverance
from the same quick kiss
prong to countless wet
dreams skewered on the love
bed prone in songs
                        of the unnamed nights
these are not things
any woman confesses
up all night
peeling off the last layer
keening
turned on the mighty
mighty wheel of desire
rocking herself
waiting on a man
stealing time
and possibilities
                        back from the images
made of mother
holding on
faith, that whisper from the islands
in the solitary still of you
a rock garden flower
a citystreet straggler
blooming in a bush of hair
with a mind for her own
                        and a body believed

White Elephant

She carries the burden of twenty rooms
on her shoulders, her arteries
swell with the obligation of heat,
energy runs virile as a rabbit,
breeding bills in a cage of worries

I count every day, every crease,
the flakes of skin that fall,
calendar to a childhood outgrown.
Adults have names for each room:
salon, parlor, sunroom, pantry.
She finds each phase in her body
in prevention magazine: psoriasis,
phlebitis, hypertension.

As they felled diseased trees from her street,
she sold her porcelain dolls to buy yelping dogs,
put bars on cellar windows to warn thieves
and the unbidden. The daughters who danced
with dad to the old 45's that the big band played *live*
                at the college formals he'd corsage her for
are gone.

Subscription to her charismatic channel
camouflages the truth:
the exorcist she seeks
is as rare as white tusk.
She knits leper bandages in endless cotton
rolls and afternoons
to send to leper colonies
where elephants wail for their fallen ones.

With no one to mourn her loss,
        strangers approach the dismantling of her white elephant,
of her life, setting it on the street for collection,
tossing the sepia ancestors into a cheap cardboard box
along with the society pages of garden parties and clubs

where their names, their chiffon skirts and orchids,
shine in aged brown tint-
as they scavenge antique fans and old coin,
writing new names in the dusty piano
where the *moonlight sonata* awaits
her arthritic hands bent
around her final will.

Cannibalism

Can you take a day apart?

one of a series
and of a woman
who makes her living sewing
in a waterfront factory, sewing shapes
of women's lips in neon, shapes that she presses
into quilted squares every day in the same spot,
walking home with leavings of lunch
and a check she passes to the man
who puts it in his clothes and up his nose, all
the while waiting
for somebody who'd challenge the lines:
>   I'd rather fish it than farm it
>   I'd rather wear it than spare it
>   I'd rather eat it than put it on the shelf

You'll see her sitting by his side in the Chevy-
he never goes out onto the Avenue
without his guitar and his gun
his body is as thin as his pipe,
he gauges impressions by the noise he leaves behind
people and tires squealing
as he revs through traffic to capture light
before dying light, like herring running
leaping furiously through a short breeding
in a polluted sea.

Boston beckons
and they carry her quilts--Mount Fuji,
Lotus Dream, in the back of the wagon
to Newbury St. where they get $150 and consignment
and head on to eat with the Vietnamese
>   sharing one of 30 varieties of steamed vegetables
with refugees who drink French coffee toothless
like beautiful Montreal girls from the far east side--
they spy the cyclist peering through his round windows

at the menu taped to the glass, reading the characters
closely--when they walk out, they pick up a squab
on the street from the boy who sells them
in a thicket of words from a van to suburbanites
who feed them to their dogs--

they drive back to the town by the river
where falls and Wampanoag ran free-
chemical warfare, cosmetic warfare
are waged there, as dredging stirs up death, and
women with crimped hair come out
of the workplace to the shopping mall
to buy products they box and mail
all day to Rome, Tokyo, New York--
they are the mortician's cosmeticians
sealing All-American images in plastic,
traipsing through their own streets looking
for a positive portrait of themselves in shop windows
                    which display reflections:

              leashes, dogs with poodle cuts and bows,
                    bait and tackle.

preyin & playin

& blowin me away
the man walks right in
lays his case at my door
starts hummin tunes
bangin on everythin in the corner

I throw a word or two in his direction,
snappin my dishcloth I say i can't help feelin
you just love to play around--
he throws that arm around my thrust-up
hip where I mostly carry the baby
and says-honey, I wanna make everything
that comes near me sing—

eat yr greens and yellows
my mama says,
this mama says
                    spit 'em out blues baby

                    spit out them blues

The Masked Man & the Mermaid

A man loped ahead of me
observing nature, wild
game as we followed
on opaque nights the road
the serpentine thread
that did lie
outside the door of our cabin

Each time we trekked out
I found a snake
dead in its skin, trapped
under tread before he could shed
it--sorry sight, he said
peering sub aqueous behind owlish frames
his red mouth the taxidermist of love.

From here the farm is the same
deal of rock, rough--
the corn still hangs from the rafters
past its season, by his longjohn
 the shape he gave it sleeping.
                    I see the neighbor's berries shelved
the gun he slaughtered the cat with
in the corner, the ceremonial band dangling
from a peg on the beam above the bed
we nailed together, the floor I stained by hand,
he stained with blood, dragging love
over it to throw into a November freeze.

I moved on Thanksgiving
from the beautybank of the Westport river
to the warmth of Fruit St. New Bedford
Portuguese house where they gave me fish--
                    Yet years later the cabin reverberates still,
timbers angling light, stamped with the force
that bends branches, with the insulation I added
abused now and his son's paraphernalia and condoms

secreted under the mattress.

I can still pick my way
the mile down, tonight I can
put one foot in front of the other.
I've spent days poised on one toe,
one angle of perspective, finding
how it works, the mechanics of direction
lucid as a beam of light.
I learned to move and fall
like a sack of fish, an object in space
seeking only toeholds,
never a part of the anchoring earth,
a mermaid
able to swim away.

I plan to stay one night
in the smoke of apple bough feeding
the belly of the stove hot
Somewhere his wife
bakes bread, bandages hurt,
follows the random throw of the dice,
is hoping for snake eyes

I avoid the tall grasses and pray
to the croupier of love
as I stake out my soul
on the bare bones of this New England plot
where even in a brutal winter
sweet jonquils on the enamel pitcher
                    center the room in a sympathy of yellows.

American Dream-Trial
o.j. and his trophies

How many hourglasses
surround the bench,
sift out ephemera
of the event, insistent
as talking drums?

How many universal microphones
air worldly-wise the innuendo
that can code blue the case?

How does the voiceless angel
banned from the courtroom
articulate that justice is as ordinary
as evil?

How do witnesses file past
with muted equivocation of sanity?
In my country "no" means
I don't remember

"Why" is a useless question, say
the victim's assistants standing
by the third ring
where the man hangs
transfigured into profile, curled lip
blood
in the city of angels
it comes down to Blood
larger than life itself, daring
to pump past everything, tracing
through the streets its epic reach
a story moving tough with the blonde climax
of where we come from, who
we be...

How many suits does it take

to screw in the light?
It's not to their advantage.

How long will the trial endure?
Until the word is bent and twisted
to fabricate a cage that captures
the pigskin hide of the American
dream crushed into reasonable
sequestration.

Home Case

The streets of america are paved with red brick
thick as your father's fist that laid them
The walls of homes have borders of birds as blue tile
so's your old lady's sight can rest

Palm trees bow to circular gardens that pool into each other
stucco statues of ancestors make like a shrine
Here in New Bedfud we have the whaleman library and the
old school of design

I went to an exhibit once and a woman in red sneakers wheeled
a shopping cart-lined with shoes, cans and bottles, and her head.

I myself prefer a man with tattoo, cane, eye patch-
Men of distinction with some personal history to them

The shelters for buses are made of fiberglass panels
they smear the rain like soft butter, I watch people through them
when they think I'm just sipping coffee

One guy named Sal wears derby like dome to cover bald spots
I like to watch him 'til the ashes meet the filter on my Winston

All that glitters is not gold, I hope he doesn't rub
my neck again and move my shaky lip that sets my cig to
dancing

When the plastic tubes that feed him are gone,
a lady with white thighs will drive him to the hotel
they have pots boiling on hotplates and cigars all day

Soon he'll be uptown in his suspenders and black flats
buying King Arthur Comix for me-
Anyone can see he's a real home case.

Piece for Four Hands

My hands crouch, cold
grey pigeons in my lap
one on each thigh
smoothing away at that damn wrinkle
in my skirt
I woke up this morning   a pigeon with one cold grey eye
staring me down from the sill
since then I've been trying to forget his face
reading Jerzy Kosinski on the fourth floor
of the Times Square Hotel to the cacophony of a drunk woman
confined here for life throwing her percussive fifth of gin
into the sharded courtyard below

I'm looking at my balding head in the mirror
I've paid for my life with my face
with my body
the scars of being born outside
the scars from giving birth inside
the stretched seams of the promise
of my children tracked over my belly
like the streets
that crisscrossed to bring me here
to a room with a bare blue bulb
and a Bible on the table
with a shower I need to lock,
         I don't care for the 400 lb. man
         who only moves from his bed to his set
         to tune in
         or the knock on my door at 3 AM

it's hard to remember
which Monday you visited
what you said that night
if you wore underwear
or how it all came off

I know I must have showed you
that national geographic my sister sent me,

     the women of the hair
     in southwest Africa
     they plait into their own hair
     the locks of lovers
     bridegrooms and brothers
     it said,
     binding through time in the patterned weave of head dress
     the story of a woman's life

The Dream of the Guide

He comes to me from the shoulders up
a fleshy, high-browed bronze moving
in diffused dark, crowned by eagle feathers,
the sigh around him complete as the last gasp
of a prisoner of conscience. He says

nothing.
I have always dreamt of having a guidance
dream, the possession of meaning in silence.
This is not the Cherokee I know, a talker
who swallows SoCo and savage cases of beer,
draws nudes on his construction site. He dreams of restoration
architecture, buys a newspaper he can't read,
saying "you got a lot to learn, and don't speak
on what you know".

They say the teacher comes when the student is ready.

I awake in my den of smoke, shadow, and old bone.
        That night I tell this one to the boys at the bar.
Dancing Dan, the pragmatic Vet, says "why not him?"
        Says he knows the lie of the land.

The Sentinel Dream

The Wampanoag comes back
chiseled, cut blunt in criminal cloth
a year later, without ceremony,
superimposed on a centerfold
of a mafia lawyer and his media wife
all smiles for the camera eye
scanning for traces of payola scandal
and therapeutic time.

The Indian does his time outside,
does not go home for supper,
is late-night, loan-shark
bagman, not the homeless kind.
He was picked for his color
and his endurance by the Family from Providence
which holds this homeport
in a heroin haze. He swears "marone"
holds a used ticket reading "poor farm"
and has their blood on his hands.
            They call him Redman.

He angles his rifle like a Minuteman
protecting a nation. He strokes
his mustache, blowing opiate smoke
rings, insinuates "not yet, you don't".
He whispers "I am the Mayor of Weld Square",
plans to meet the Drug Czar when he visits.

I must be having a lucid dream:
I reach out to take the packet of Power
from his small fist, wondering how
can a shark in the richest port on the coast
            circuit have so few teeth.....

Dancing with the Serial Killer

while the girl who idolized you
stood home looking into her glass
cage of newts and tropical fish
I packed my curious flesh
into navy sweats
slid down the balustrade of the historic house
into the night, arranged myself into a heap
on the front seat of your Buick
jammed the tape as far as it would go
on head music
pushed the Greek worry beads out of the rear view
as you pulled through the stop sign
rushing to be ahead of your time........

I wanted to be a head of my time
taking it in through my skin tingling
the way your lover's friends do their drugs,
like a car does a curb in collision,
we're arrested in mid-flight
by the hit-man of poetry on the corner
        handing out epithets funded by the lottery:
"thanks for poems we can profit by"
he says, his latest touches base
with history, a note on the serial killer
who sliced through providence, r.i.,
mincing steps, crying "let's go crazy" in all the gay bars
as victim women wrote his epitaph.
It says they've found him, slight and high
wending his way through a dance floor,
moving to a boy gyrating in a cage
asking "what can I wear to my birthday orgy?"

The hit man sidles to us, a crab without claws,
        where once we thought him wild we know he's merely
crazy--we're not that kind of animal, we chant in unison-but
the ignition doesn't spark and soon we're trapped
on Cottage Street by the gang rape parade:

young and old women in black polyester,
black babushkas, carrying banners reading
"Justicia Crucifada" in the name of love
for fellow immigrants who drank and watched
and banged the bar or the woman on the pool table.

They don't know this is the cruising zone, heading
down court street, past the House of Corrections.
They respond to the Women's Center vigil with
wispy candleflame of their own mission
in the name of love that leashes them to dead weight
of potato diets and clocks marking wages
in decimal digits.
I smile at the girl who passes the window
in a matronly second of the original shift
she turns out all day: "we are lovers, not fighters"
she explains the motive-she knows me from the
Cape Verdean News and thinks I am covering this
and not living my life
We join the fringes to watch, escaping the hit-man
        leafleting those who don't read English

Remember? spying Joe Thomas on top of city hall
behind the flag, targeting for a patch of light
in all this religious energy, camera ready to choose
what will be recalled: Is he aiming for the stitchers
with their bad eyes and black cat-glasses from community
opticians or at a fish cutter
in rubber boots and oily bandana?
We'll read about it tomorrow in small print
alongside what's supposed to make us happy:
        a bottle of juice, a piece of meat,
        a belly full

You don't have to be telepathic
to see providence leap anywhere in a flash
connecting to the fever
like a negative charge--
let's blow this town and Be There, you said

we pass through kinetic night on an interstate
releasing ourselves to cold leather--"That's the kind
of animal they are" you smile and gun the engine
in a still-cold machine.
I expect we'll be at the club soon.

Dear R.,
I send this to you working in a hospice
with a new sequence of death, numbers the astrologers
couldn't calculate when they divided the heavens into
futures,
numbers your lover didn't include when he counted himself-
I suspect you know we both danced with the serial killer
at some point and still may
unless he watches us, incandescent in the hot flash
of his emotions, leaning against the bar,
processing images slowly
        the way killers Polaroid the remains.

I've updated this postscript to you twice:
they've found six sets of bones
scattered past the tree line on I-95.
Expendable blood?
Spring is here.
The air is strangely fragrant.
Will you find time to write
and tell me who's going to sponsor this city?
        Who's going to move the space around here?

Sacred Ground

Cornplanting Moon--Spring, it begins
                    Here,

Debra Medeiros, 29;

Nancy Paiva, 36;

Debra Greenlaw DeMello, 35;

Dawn Mendes, 25;

Rochelle Clifford Dopierla, 28;

Robbin Rhodes, 29;

Mary Rose Santos, 26;

Sandra Ann Botelho, 25;

        number nine....number nine...number

Christina Monteiro, 20, Sandra's cousin missing...

Gayle Botelho, 32, desaparecida 11/3/88,
tattoo: the butterfly and the black rose

here in america is the night watchman
the vigilante of the angry
parent, the power-god allied with scorching
summer rotting flesh to detritus

Freeze-Up Moon—Fall

        Hunters return and families are reunited.

November is the blood month-

The mango-moon bloats,
the scorpion sidles
from under his stone.

They have discovered six sets of bones.
These missing persons need to be identified
and their families contacted.

We plunder one another
as soundbridge, we struggle
among the lines, the lies,
          and the lying there.

None of These Women

The custodians of court ask me "Who do you represent?"
I want to say God. Instead
I watch the jury box from behind my rail
stuffed with media betting
that feverish frenzy might breed an event.
The judge hasn't been bought out
by the Cuban drug lord.

the D.A. prances to tape-time--
his rep was made on rape, heard 'round the world,
Big Dan's bar: one victim, many perps, shaved and
suited, transformed to respectable image he saw
through and prosecuted to the wrath of his Portuguese kin

today's litany tolls many victims, one accused,
a fleshy lawyer counteracting expectation, hangs onto
his cocaine-crumpled life,
denies pubic evidence in this crime
          of bagged hair and bone.

A chain of dusky boys are run through the room in handcuffed
passage,

their faces freezing like righteous citizens in a stick-up,
moving on this auction block in ripped jeans,
naked from the waist up.

I hallucinate the haggard face of a dead woman hovering over the
bench.
We at court create her story since
none of these women witness justice
today, testify to spirit stolen.

None of these women got death
        that would affect an estate
None of these women got death
that fed their images into inky
eulogy on the citypress
None of these women got death
beyond a file in the Times morgue.

All of these women were missing
and no law came looking
All of these women were missing
labeled like a rare species
All of these women were missing
names on white paper,
said "prostitute and drug addict"

the highway slayer knows
all of these women were desperate

the highway killer knows
all of these women were ailing

the serial killer knows
all of these women were sisters
with no close kin
        their tribal joys jabbed under the skin
sisters despised and taught no skills

sisters dumped as roadside kill

None of these women assumed their right,
none of these women challenged the system,
none of these women could buy protection
none of these women could claim their necessary
roots & names

Some of these women had no photos
Some of these women had no teeth
All of these women's remains filled baggies
      All of these were victims of the street

None of these women can rise to their own story
None of these women are not our destiny

If we choose to deny our choices
if we escape the reality
that we must forget the curses
or gentility we've heard
and brave the language
to begin again: Word
to the Mother in us all,
dare for the rapture
of a goddess call
to move past the sweats of privilege and shame
and grasp our resemblance, our value…
      our names

Vampires

So, bear them here, the suspects:

predators trolling the streets
ring around the rosy block
gamin' in a rite of Spring:
      the man who scales and guts fish,
      the deplorable stone crusher,

      the porn-video king flying from beach to beach,

the addicted lawyer and his seedy deals,
the scarred children in adult skins, sticking it
to sacred symbols, the defilers
of Freetown Native America State Forest,
the suicidal batterers boozing to sounds that
spit and rock the rage, the profane ordinary
evil repeating "the worst is more than you deserve"

Take one last good look at yourself
scrawls the magician on the mirror
at the foot of the stairs.
The Nosferatu, this non-person,
this assassin, has no reflection in the mirror
        blind to beauty in another's eyes.
He wears the mask of sanity, sacrificing
each pump of heart to keep it going,
trades sleep for trophies, the intimate
objects of desire.

Hawk-like, penetrating, telescoping vision,
the magician knows the Nosferatu on the street:
he circulates ardent as the blood of the women
he pursues next, the wolf with the red throat,
shifting a tropic wish into tundra waste
        with the twist of his howl into history.

Queen of the Underworld

I came up on Ascension Street
my father an honest fisherman
my mother an absentee
my first pimp named me Crystal
liking the ring and the purity

he went by Bobby Pagan
they called him Doctor, too
'til we did up all we copped

discarded more than we drew

My husband they call Blackjack
he owns two bars and a laundry
says I can't use it if I can't smoke it
bought our cars with bags of weed

what I own hangs loose around my neck
gold to hypnotize these guards
you call this place a shelter
        on the street that ain't the word

I was livin' in a sanctuary
house, now it's a shootin' gallery
some say folks workin' welfare money
I say look at your destiny

somethin' breakin' inside me, honey
when the Volunteers take away my food
and the counselor calls me an f--bitch
when I come in late for curfew

I'm doin' this for Venus,
she's comin' on the weekend
        we're gettin' ourselves a section 8
in the town with a beach and friends

I went to the AA meetings
and I talked in the women's group
didn't know how to stay the man with the gun
    who'll set me up as his dupe

    say, won't you take this pink sweater
    lace just ain't my style
    that shade is exactly your color
            ...now, let me sweep these aisles.

the last supper

how could you foresee
scattered glasses, bloody beds,
empty rooms in a shooting
gallery when you bought
the print of Central American peasants
sharing bread in a blue-red container
of light, a casa? Each character is a color,

and it's jesús' birthday here
in a disemboweled house
where graffiti's scrawled
on the hanging wall, desiderata
posters ripped by the gang
of suicidal revolutionaries
who hit the mattresses.

You delivered the package
the day after the latin feast
where circuits of men with hats
secreted rice between their teeth,
knives under their hats. There were tears
in your eyes scanning rooms dusted
with the incense of immigration faces,
lost again to the streets. You must sweep
and clean broken furniture, hands
in the storehouse of memory signing
never, no more. You must be radiant
in hell's kitchen like bread in the oven,
like a sparrow beating wings furiously
in the winds.

The Green Room

Waiting in the green room
for the show to begin,
here is your host:

a gaunt, high-collared woman
sits on the window ledge in a sliver of sun
through frost-stars, balancing a pencil
like the boys in the backroom do their cues,
staring hard at the arch and the arrival
of a short, get-back woman in denim

here is the guest:
fixes one brown eye on the eraser
and one brown foot toward the fire escape,
says "I got a brother at Brown who's comin'
tonight with my stuff", remembers the two tall
sisters with rings visiting the time this social
worker was green: presents of cool Vicks
VapoRub, pistachio ice cream, cartons
of Kools; today she has Newport 100's,
matchstick boats from Joe on Deer Island,
a snapshot of Neecee poking through
her sunsuit at Paragon Park

The script says : "Betty Mack" but like her street name, it ain't
Real

The energy:
lances through the passage
                lacing the lobby to classic strains:
            "the dark whore of Brazil weeps, mornings
                        matter little"

Betty is the designated client,
she knows the drill--nods to the rhythm,
is led down the corridor past photos
of rough-housing people smiling

from the construction paper collage
labeled *light after d.a.r.c.:*
jimmy love's lips, mikey's grin,
ro's arms around parky's middle,
caught in the only free time   & learnin group
where survival wasn't a packet
and Thursday was rib day every week.

She enters the office, a closet scrubbed
as work detail and used on Mondays
by doc from the rox.
It still stinks of Lysol and he stinks
of gin, waiting with record and probes,
as the door closes and one of many flies
on the wall lands on her meatless frame
tied into a mint johnny, open to screen
for contraband.

Slow Sashay

We watched your comings and goings
short pants and long spikes,
purring over Scrabble like Eartha
Kitt practiced over nights walking
your tattooed head through the streets,
slipping your alias, a commercial
fragrance we'd pickup at Filene's
steps from where you sold the essence.

You're hiding out here for months
escaping the Cadillacs of brothers who chase
women like money. Their thin license
plates pronounce *in God We Trust*, vanity
spells out over town
where we live.

"Callin me,
from the Old World callin
me slow sashay,
takin me Out,
a mama even tells her girl
'why can't you be more like her?'

this neck of Hoo-do
charms is my protection. I've put
my goddamned life on the line every day,
I wanted men to die for me"

This country won't take kindly
to your books on spells of love.
You have no girlfriend who understands
the gardener from San Juan the way you do,
flashing his red underwear through your dreams.

"I can always tell the kind of man, even
inside the walls. I'm saving these passes
to trade in for cigarettes, and them to sell

to get me out and over. I'm fixin to have
the operation. Then nobody even try to
call me Hector. I'll be sister
on the street and off".

for Jesús from El Salvador on the bus reading Newsweek
for Freddie Savoie

When I was a girl
I climbed stairs wide as sideboards
to my cousin's mahogany,
shuttered room
I thought the shape of the world
came in the vapors
from the cut-glass bottles on the dresser
I read the names aloud
to myself from the tags around the necks:
Tabu My Sin Intimate
each stressed last syllable
savored like the furtive sound
in a world where I laid out on a canopied bed
at thirteen Louise's treasure:
carafes with wings, patent bags and pink shoes

Miles away under flags in brown buildings
worked girls and boys whose mothers said seriously
"carry your honor high"
the mission was a trip with a purpose
"Salvation through work" carved over one gate--
Louise first showed me the camps in Life
magazine's profile of Red Cross health workers
visiting one "rehab" years before the finality
of the solution and mountainous
                          evidence: 348,820 shoes
                                 42,555 shoes
                              13, 694 carpets
            I know a grossmutter who carried her oriental
                in the night tightly as swaddling on the ferry
                                 to freedom
            "father said do not leave anything so important
                                    behind"

She still lives in New England
where she walks her tethered cats in the park
with its sculpture of a fist huge
enough to reach heaven with the prayers
of survivors and the names of the lost---they tread streets
researching mailboxes looking for her name and her kind,
finding instead rain-splattered copies of Newsweek
where Berlin lawyers argue an exaggeration,
a sensationalism, a media lie about the Event-

She married a survivor sheltered from pain
under a false name adopted
in the Catholic orphanage weeks before
betrayal of his mother to the trains--
"not all objects were expendable
as the people" she told me:
consider the lucky aryan family
who shared the same monogram
as the Jews that were led away
as vermin,
and so kept their linen.

I see her from the street, lounging
in the half-light shadow of grape vine, pear tree
re-collecting the generations
poised like the Maja contessa waving her fan
as though she didn't need it to atomize the air
around her heavy with the desires
of men with full stomachs digging wide trenches cheered on
by women waving handkerchiefs

I call for an update from time to time
Many times she has had to locate a gas leak, "I think I smell gas"
she says, even in my tenement flat
the litany of names is carved in memoriam
when disease is an issue
beyond ashes: like agent
                    orange, Xyclon B,
                    dyes distilled like people

beyond recognition and naming

Joan Didion writes of El Salvador:
> found in Mexicanos--bodies and faces, over years,
> and I can list it, list it, list it
> found in Antiguo Cuncatlan el dia 24 de marzo '82,
camison de dormir celeste (a nightshirt the color of celestial
sleep)

Jesus,
the names are numbered
these numbers are our names
these numbers are roster of our days
these numbers in phrases are exponential equations calling us
to draw on our highest powers
and Holocaust
like last breath
remains a word
driven by an empty wind

WACO   April 18, 1993

pacing with cold coffee,
we wait for the mechanic
to adjust our brakes, shock
absorbers, watching the light
screen green ghosts through the t.v.
as a compound goes up in smoke--
my g.g.generation, the rock-and roll
Koresh cabal sucking childhood and memory
from another city-on-a-hill hallucinating
its terrible, karma-scarred sacrifice-
the wind flutters the DEA colors in our face
and the sirens wail--
on the other side of town, families disunited
wait in stations, flying to messianic Oprah or Phil
after their baggage clears inspection
to speak on this alien-nation

Today
the Chief of State ate at a Holocaust memorial
and his Empress proclaimed her accountability-
History you'll find in an old book with gilded binding, or
rewinding itself through time on a screen
—death in the House—
catching what's been sculpted Somewhere else by unseen hands,
spoken of only by voiceless angels

how it goes…

herons sing
nightwatch brings you in
serenaded through leaded gauze
wooed by the cackle of old bone

Poetic Drama

THE BURGUNDY LETTERS

for John Emigh-who loved the theater and New Orleans
and for Joli Gonsalves-who loved the rhythm of this play

SETTING: COFFEEHOUSE IN NEW YORK CITY; GAMBLING
DEN IN NEW ORLEANS

CHARACTERS:
THEDA (BILLIE)
GIRL
DELLA
UNCLE HAL
JIMMY LOVE
HECTOR
MAMA
WHITE MAN

ACT I

The stage is divided equally down the middle into two separate
areas with a common backdrop allowing for variations on the
theme common to both sets. It is an impressionistic mural of the
railroad and those who worked it. The design is powerful, anti-
representational, neither modern nor old, and captures the
feeling of that movement.
Behind the backdrop is a high staging set up like a horizontal
balcony/scaffolding that traverses the stage on which are enacted
scenes from the phantom pasts of the characters in both sets.
The set viewed in Act I is the one stage left. It is a small, folksy
coffeehouse: wooden floor boards, round wooden tables with
checkered cloths and globular candles. It is dimly lit by overhead
clusters of bare bulbs shedding a golden hue over all. The few
tables are scattered mostly near the left wall hung with shells and
floats. The performance is over--the audience gone. The
ashtrays cradle smoked cigarettes. Some tables have programs
left on them and one has a harmonica. The table far right has two

seated patrons: the woman, **Theda**, sitting near the implied wall, diagonally facing the audience, and the **Girl** sitting with her back angled to the audience, almost diagonally opposite the woman.

The woman, **THEDA,** is in her late 50's, well-worn and thin. She doesn't necessarily look older than her age, but she looks every bit of it. She is dressed in a long tweed-like overcoat that is large for her, possibly a man's coat, under which we can view a nubby grey sweater frazzled with age and a pair of forest green polyester "stretch pants" with those ugly seams that stand in relief like scars. Her shoes are also emblematic--dark sneakers of nondescript brand whose edges roll in on themselves with overuse and are tangible clues to the shape that she's in which her decorous slouch camouflages. Her hands reveal her, too: fingers cigarette-stained and skin worn from service. Her fingers are slow and belabored as they reach for cigarettes or play with the small old-fashioned change purse in front of her. She sometimes plays with it to hear near-mute melody. She also plays with the small rose pin she's secreted on the underside of her lapel, a memento of a past time she clings to and wants no one to steal. Occasionally, she will smooth down the net kerchief, tied at an odd angle, which she wears over her flattened grey hair.

THEDA is accompanied by **GIRL.** She is a student, sporting a delicate sweater with tiny colored bows down the front and a pair of designer jeans. A new tweed blazer hangs on the back of her chair. She has placed a tape recorder on the table between the two women. She is the oral-monitor of life. She has planned to tape the whole evening. She will check her machine at the beginning of Act I to ensure it is still running, but will turn it off at the beginning of Act II, finding it impossible to monitor Theda's life. She serves as a sounding board and mirror. She fiddles with the machine and responds to Theda's story with attention, emotion and reaction. Her role as signifier for a host of observations is important to the audience. Her body language reveals and mirrors them!
Throughout the play there will be music playing at intervals from the jukebox in the center of the fishnet wall. Act I is introduced with Dolly Parton's rendition of Hank Williams' "You Never Can Tell" which Girl begins to tape.

All the songs are country or blues songs--T.Bone Walker's "How Long, Baby, How Long" can be used in Act I or Act II to augment feeling, rhythm, and tone. They are intended to evoke timeless place and time here is measured by speech which is the ritualistic exorcism of Theda's experience.

Music plays--**GIRL** switches on recorder as soon as she realizes this might be "historical and important", but the music ends abruptly in middle of the song and **THEDA** begins to fill in the space:

THEDA: O.K.
I guess I can talk to you a bit
but you know I can't miss my train
I take it every Friday at nine
the A train to Columbus Circle
uptown to Johnson's
and my friend, there, Alice
she gives me the biggest box of barbecue
leftovers of the night
but always something special, too
tea with whiskey sometimes
and a taste of that island stuff,
when her boy has a notion
to bring it by

GIRL: (timidly) What happened to the music?

THEDA: Dont'cha worry, girl! Lissen now first
off, my name is Theda
but everybody calls me Billie
my mama loved Valentino and thought she
was Theda
and named me after her
she was the gypsy, my mama
what with her bangles and orange shawl
dripping of fringe
sitting and rocking
by the hour
by the window   in Waycross

Mama carries her rocking chair to balcony area and sits in
it. She is a Creole lady with large earrings, a head kerchief, and
a flamboyant dress. She hums a blues tune softly to herself,
as though there was nobody in the world but her and her reverie.
She has a far-away look, is beautiful even in the inexpensive
frock and too-bright lipstick.

MAMA: my baby
(repeat 3 times)
done left me
my baby ..where is ya, baby
where is you now..I didn't want to give you up
but they made me, baby
said it was for the best, so you could eat
and go to a fine school, oh
done gone..

THEDA: In those times they thought
she crazed, dreamin' away the half-time
she wasn't haulin'
they pulled me away from her quick
you can believe it
my mama kep' me from work, I stay
home stitchin into bits of cloth
red rosy hearts and flower borders
and winkin jack-o'-diamonds
I remember all them faces
and the names we 'broidered in
for those gone by: Lemuel, Ruth, Tobias
Mercy
and bible words mama was fond of: bless the
Lord, o my soul, and later
god of vengeance hear my prayer deliver me
and playing with her saints
with their pretty faces
all lost on goin' to heaven
yes, ma'am...
goin for walks with herself, that's what
mama called herself
after the way of the man

who fathered me
a scot whose people
come from the high land
goin' for walks in the underbrush,
through all bramble
getting caught and wriggling to come undone
and catch up to mama's long legs.
that was the learnin' I did
how to do a sampler simple and even,
how to tell the poison fruit from the clear

WHITE MAN:
appears on upper balcony--backs towards
Mama-dressed in suit, hat, cigar--booming
and business-like tone conveys authority:

we have contracted long enough
with them-if they don't sign today
we'll go ahead and make them pay !

THEDA: work didn't do me much
chile 'most half my age
shuckin' me--they knew I didn't know
what they did, didn't want to--
the only things i wanted was OUT
living with aunt, a real crazy woman
always mad at everybody
she wouldn't put out a nickel or a kind word
without scratchin' the old buffalo
or the niceness on her memory-she
was very nice
sweeter than honey and twice as thick
and nothin' I ever tole her ever got past
her reFinement
this with mama raggedy, living on potatoes
and the notions of aunt
I hated that woman who forgot her own:
she even called me "po' wafo'"
when I started seein boys, well,
she hated me worser--I

114

never did nuthin just sit and talk
walk round the garden
not even touchin hands
her whole thang with me
was 'bout jealousy
'bout mama bein' independent, not having
no husband underfoot and never scared
of anybody else
neither—

THEDA reaches for a cigarette and lights it as she continues:

me just like mama
it was too much for Della to take
any mo', I tole her I was pregnant
that was the worst sin, she believed that lie,
started her whinin', pedalin' it faster and faster
like she allus did til she bayed
louder and longer than she ever did.
I knew that was the end
and I felt sorry for her I guess
gave her a sampler I turned out
special for her
for the occasion
it said "Be still and know
that I am god"
from the hymnal you know
underneath "Theda, 1939"

--cut to scene on scaffolding as lights go almost out on stage-
Della takes shape: she drips fat; she has food stains on the
apron that covers the front of her large housedress; she is the
essence of gluttony. She wipes her hands on the apron and picks
the sampler out of the hands of a small, dusty adolescent girl that
is **BILLIE** (Young Theda). Dusty hair, dusty clothes, dusty
skin all suggest the poor "mulatto" status granted her in this
racist environment.

DELLA: You really put yourself
into this, Billie dear but

you must know how to spell--
Huh?

BILLIE: I'm sorry. What do you mean?"

DELLA: You have "no" 'stead of "k n o w"

BILLIE: It's the thought that counts, ain't it?

Della frowns, disgusted, and walks away shaking her head.

BILLIE: That's what I wish I'd settled for with you.
just the thought
        (spotlight dims as we move from scaffold to stage)

THEDA: 'Course I knew she wouldn't like it
she was the kind that never do
know how to take things,
love to give--advice to every body,
lectures to me
but never could hold a gift
without wonderin' if it would splinter
in her hand, or without thinkin
when duty would call her again
to loosen them purse strings
With me
she didn't even see duty's devil
horns proddin her to say
somethin----
My thought was hightailin
freefloatin', there was nothin'
to keep me fixed

to that nitty-gritty
not hate or pity or kin.
These names cropped up in my head-
New Orleans, Memphis, St. Petersburg,
'Lanta--they had come from tales heard
second-time around, from mama's dreams,
Ring Lardner stories and Life magazine-

In mama's plaid shift, a pack of handrolleds
in one pocket and six dollars in the other
I held no particular one in mind
but notions in my head handy to try
out in any of 'em
led on by mama's bright wings—

GIRL checks tape recorder, changes tape to side 2, and places
her jacket over her shoulders for warmth. **THEDA** offers her
a cigarette which she politely declines. **GIRL** rises to get coffee
out of the unplugged urn. She pours two cups and....
Lights move to mauve tone but **THEDA** doesn't blow out
the candle on the table although she cradles it for warmth and
vague comfort.
Lights dim

End of ACT I

ACT II

We are introduced to the second set on the stage as the lights
slowly reveal the outlines of that portion of the stage located
stage right. What was indiscernible before is now known to be the
fourth wall--one of loose meshed net--through which we view action
as through a veil. This net is a continuation, physically and
technically, of the fishnet wall of the coffeehouse. It slinks around
the front of half the stage and wraps it down back the other side,
enveloping this portion of the stage as a cage.
Beyond the facade we see a small gambling den: a card table set
up for a game. The game is undetermined for the evening: we
have dice and cards and chips. Whatever game it is will fall in the
shadow of the railroad backdrop. The red lighting that illumines
the set and the presence of the cardboard "madame" of this place,
Miss Sally, as she peers down from her painted visage on the left
wall behind the net announcing "Miss Sally's House of Cards: I
Read Them--the Rest Is Up to You!) set the mood.

Spot on **JIMMY LOVE** sitting on a wooden crate, low at the
table. He is small and agile, dressed in a three-piece suit, flashy
as he is fast. He sports shiny leather shoes, has a scarf and
fedora on the back of his chair. He is about 35, lightly bearded,

and projects money. His pinky ring, diamond studs, and easy
laughter betray his emotional values which begin and end with his
pleasure.
He slaps his thighs musically and calls out the names of the streets
in New Orleans in a singsong voice to a tune
of his own device:

JIMMY LOVE:
Pigeon Town, Girttown, Calliope, Black Pearl,
Apricot, Apple, Ramparts, Fern,
Melpomene, Terpsichore, Thalia, Dauphine,
Prytania, Carondelet, , Burgundy,
Bourbon, Real........

Lights move to encompass the two men seated at the table.
They have a bottle and a basket of chicken and each has a
half-full drinking glass. As he ends his song, we hear
"Outskirts of Town" bluesy with harmonica and see
HECTOR. We know he is tall not only from his size but
by spying his long legs under the table. He is well-built and
muscular, late 40's, wearing velveteen pants of a rich
burgundy color, a leather belt, and a blousy shirt with wide
sleeves. The shirt hangs off one shoulder and reveals a
tattoo erasure, i.e., a scar where the name once was and
tracings of the once-bold entwined snakes.
He is attractive in a magnetic way without being
handsome: his restrained force is evident and can be
off-putting. He is sitting back in his chair and tossing the
dice to amuse himself. His Creole background is in his
lilting accent:

HECTOR: Hey, man, she was slo' and lo'
ya know what I mean
she took me down the curves
slick as they been with such femaleness
now I'm tellin' you
Mabie and me, we're through-
from now on 'Cinda is my woman

JIMMY LOVE: Phhh! Bet!

You ain't right, you never right
How many times you said it before
It was Mabie who threw you out the door!
You can't hold your gin, then you can't keep
yo' woman--you need womens,
like me, two, three a night
'til you get past that little girl
from the hills--here, have a bite
of this chicken so's you can drink some more
you can't keep trippin' just to even the
score-

HECTOR: you don't know what you say, J.,
she's never on my mind
what game'll it be tonight--black
jack by candlelight?

JIMMY LOVE: yah, that's me all over,
black jack it is and you deal,
if I believe your lie you'll tell me another
so I don't-it's Theda who's for real!

Hector shakes his head, starts to deal. As music plays
we follow light to stage left and stage right is bathed
from a deep red to blacklight.
THEDA and **GIRL** are sitting have been sitting in
candlelight but now are fully illuminated.

THEDA: I'm thinkin' south, I'm feelin' home
and no place was more home to me than N.O.
New Orleans Louisiana
N.O.L.A.
This time of year when I'm waitin' on spring
I remember those names
of flowers and fruit
and things you'd like to eat
they sounded so good, rounded
like they waz on the tongue
That's how it was when i came into nola,

back then--that patchy old road,
bright as a quilt with light--
no flowerin things, bein winter yet
how the light caught up that land
all the little dogeared
squares the color of ripe watermelon
and clover, and the lost lime
bottom of something
I had never seen before, the sea
Coming in first thing i saw was Pontchartrain
big as Jehosapath
like god's wading pool, stuck
at the bottom of all that sky
sky so big, sky coming down like diamonds,
meeting the trees, just breakin
then, in little triangles
of ash and blonde.
This was something for me,
a wonder to me.
Here i was from a little pocket
tucked away in Georgia where the earth
crumpled in my hand
when I tried to turn over a garden...and
the sky slung so low
like a lid on a clay jar.
I felt I never could breathe right.
But Nola, that was "it".
Like we said, "it" was the appeal
you know
and the freedom to be
any body, could breathe
you know
"it" was sure here and I was feelin
I had found it, easy as i wanted it,
like that ol' slow river

or mebbe sweet and slick as
the sea-licked road, leading me to nola,
pulling me through all them curves.
Everybody to home heads on to nola

if they head on anywhere
Even Uncle Hal, dried out as he was
b'lieved....

move to scaffolding where **Uncle Hal** is seen where **Della**
once was...she is now on far side of scaffolding, sitting and
knitting, hanging her legs over side--He is hanging out of
dusty green overalls and wears work boots. He is leaning
on his hoe and talking to the audience but "over their heads"
to the click of Della's needles in the distance—

HAL: I b'lieve
if ya wanna pull farther and faster
you gotta hitch up to that city
yessir, that's the place
to make good and shine
...and if you only get to shine at night
huh, like some of them ladies
'least you can do it in black sateen...
(licking his lips) s'promised land,
it's the waters of life (holding his hoe between his
arms like a woman)
an ocean of likkers
and places..for men...to relieve themselves
of their cash and "cupid's weight"

DELLA: ...Hal!...Oh...(plaintive, helpless)

HAL: ..as the tea set ladies call it (lowered tone)
Comin', Della....
                              (fade out)

THEDA: Anyways
I got there
started railroadin
pickup drivers,
showin' my legs, I reckon
always waz real good, best thang about me--
and look where they been!
Well, I rode in the backsfullup with boys, up

front on the runnin board when they waz full up.
Lots o' rides--
people makin' short hauls in them days,
for food, for chil'ren, for fun...
not like folks now with no spaces
in between
...and glad for me too
'surprised to see a gal
doin' it, haulin' her own
chile nowadays got no chance
chance--too many dopes on the road
lookin' for cash, and crazies, too,
honey let me tell you
this town ain't fit
ya'll better go home
before ya end up hustlin',
pardon me, yo ass
from that pizz' parlor 'cross the street
girls pretty as you
gettin' spit out by this city every day
even that looker
with hair the color of midnight
eyes blue as the tassels on the robe o' Jesus
she got taken up
with somebody pimpin' off her pretty soft
back--an eats not good here--
coffee dirtier than the Mis'sippi
no chicory to liven it up, meat
tougher than rawhide

GIRL--shuts off tape recorder-she buttons her jacket
and shuffles in seat as though readying to leave if
tbis keeps up--yet she is riveted to Theda's eyes
and intensity. She is less dainty now, nervously
slurping coffee as Theda continues.

THEDA: Nola, yeah, that was heaven
(she reaches for cig, jingles her change purse,
smiles for first time)
...and can't talk natch'ally 'bout it

without talkin' 'bout hector
hector was my first friend in Nola
and then my best, and for a long time
after too....
he was a bourbon street reg'lar
things weren't different then than now
new folks always suckered by that part o'town
all that jazz, ya know
jazz such a dirty word, not proper
t'all to speak in those times
but fit that place to a T.

Well, I come in
there I waz tired from all that truckin'
soppin' wet from the afternoon
showers they alus have there
and smack in the middle of more color
folks than i ever seen--
women the color of coffee light with cream
babies the color of fawn
young boys the color of burnt toast
girls with knees nubby as pecans
in the middle of the circle they made
was a man darker than me
blacker than any body
so black he was light
so black he shone and anything
they throwed at him--fists, insults, women,
sin--would roll right off
not touchin' him at all
standin' there in lean velveteen
in one of them pretty shirts with creole sleeves
he could've been a picture
but I knew he surely wasn't
He had an eye so sly
I swear that even after i knew him
that eye was like a hand hanging on
to my collar that i couldn't shake off--
when i say eye
I do mean eye

hector had one real eye, one glass
he'd gotten his self into a bar-fight
been knifed by a drunk,
sailor, he had to walk around without
any lovin' if ya know what I mean,
Po' fella had to be sutured up
and left nola forever--
but hector, his rep survived
for years on that one thang.
Anyways I'm gettin
ahead of myself here
when I first seen him he was lookin'
down with his real eye at a snake
wrapped around his middle like some fancy belt
talking some mumo jumbo--mambusu se mambusu se
some such and venhese eh the snake

would be rockin' on the upbeat
then he'd slide into action
coilin' 'round Hector
light on scaffold where **HECTOR** is wrapped in a
small boa--**JIMMY LOVE** is shaking a tambourine, singing
"Travelin' Shoes" ("I ain't ready to go, no,no, no..I ain't
put on my travelin' shoes, Lord")

HAL and **BELLA** stand at one end of the scaffold, staring
at the spectacle. Bella points with her knitting needle and
Hal is wide-eyed.

HECTOR: (speaking to snake as friend,
dancing and moving intimately with it):
mambusu se vanese se
mambusu eh vanese eh
arabou ke le pah
ven'conmihiho
yah!

THEDA: Every chantin' brought a new move
and the crowd gettin' quieter even as
it got bigger-some would throw money

silver dollars, gold pieces--that
was rent money in the day
I have seen men
up and down that street dancin' for money
singin' for money
struttin' for money
but he was the only one
wrappin' a snake around him
like a lover for money--
this went on for a bit,
who knows how long it had been goin' on,
before i found it out
I ain't seen nuthin' like it
anywhere
ever
that man was an original
alright
and I got
more stories outta him
than I kin tell--
he done my biznes some good -if
you want more I'll give
you more
but I think somethin to eat
right about now
would be fine--don't you

Lights Dim as both stand, **Theda** stretching and **Girl**
heading for the snack table.

End of Act II

Act III

Stage right moves from its long blacklit status to full
lighting, revealing **JIMMY LOVE** and **HECTOR**
sitting with bowls of food in front of them. The net in
front of that portion of stage is gone, revealing them
clearly. We can also see a door behind where they
are sitting, leading off of the room. It is a heavy door

divided down the middle by an art nouveau lily out of
whose petals issue two words that demarcate the portions
of that door: "Chastity" on one half, "Charity" on the
other.

JIMMY LOVE: don't you just love that door
heavy and richlookin'
I'd like to split that door down the middle
have the part with chastity on it over my bath
and the part with charity
over my bed...if I had me...

HECTOR: now lokka this
soup and beans
no good, no good
nola usta give me oysters on the corner
plump and pink and grey
po' boys so thick, so's i couldn't even get
my mouth round 'em..

JIMMY LOVE: don't sound like no oystas to me-sounds like...
you been holdin' out on me, man! (laughing)

HECTOR: been some dog's while
since i shined my beam on any body-followin
her home from jackson square
layin on her how she could bloom at night
prettier than any moonflower..
seems some time...
seems only once before
I did it up right

JIMMY LOVE: Billie? that again?

HECTOR: Now I've heard 'nuf 'bout that self to
last-
I was sitting here playin with them dice
'fore you come in and talkin jus' like you
was here...didn't matter if you was or
not, the story be the same..

how i was down deep in love
if she was crosseyed at me
everythin changed faster than a devil
moon--she
was powerful with me, I say
I'd sit havin' tea with my man then,
c.w., and c.w. he starin at me, I'd be
sayin' nuthin' and nuthin' all mornin'
some say, ya cain't have heaven
without a hell...
I kin see that!

JIMMY LOVE: I never seen that--seen you mad
and quiet, though, yeah, that waz
mad, in them days, so quiet
and turned into yo'self
she couldn't even put on her old show
to make you laugh--nuthin worked
with them black moods....yeah, and
then
chasin' that woman 'round her own house
for wearin' red outside it,
throwin' out her blouse held up with lil'
pink bows...shoooo'......
I been figurin'
all these years how hard it musta been
for ya holdin all that feelin in,
so's ya wouldn't blow sky high...
(slaps hector on the back)
Guess i forgot ya did let some out..
some days, some ways!

HECTOR: (slowly, reflectively)
she'd tussle with herself about how she looked
paintin' in her wide mouth to pout and eyes to look
a wild cat...'stead o' the kitten she was
never fooled me
from where we rode over to Gretna on the ferry
that first day...what with everybody in this world
fixin' everybody, believin' in power like that

in gettin' it over some body in some game
hunters chasin' themselves in their kills' eyes
She had power the woman
she be thinkin' it was me and never tole her
different --Hector had the power alright,
it wasn't in the snake neither
it was in the eyes of themselves
        in what I seen there, their wantin
more, not havin no rest
shyin away or tearin you down
hector knew each eye was different
and the only true seein with both of 'em closed
meetin' each face fresh-touched
with the lovin', yeah,
and the deepest, down, drag-me-up-from-down
and-rock-me lovin was that woman
an how she smiled so easy on everybody seein
how the magic was how any body
could be grandmere lachaise
who they'd hang for murder,
or po' andre the young cure they fixed back then

JIMMY LOVE: Don't you fall behind all that rememberin'
you needs you some skin against skin to
be right...man, it was Hector they was comin
to see, it was hector that met 'em in his gold
waistcoat...full of it, from the shirts women made
for him to their sweet talk,
full of the skin you could see right through
to the soul,
Hector!

Hector is in a trance, staring at "Miss Sally". Jimmy Love
shakes him repeatedly, and he starts coming out of it.

HECTOR: Green is the healin'
she allus said....green is the healin'

JIMMY LOVE: Hector! come out of it.
You're here now-this is the mil....

Hector!
Lawd! Where....?

His appeal trails off and the we fade out to a violet light.
Stage right is now bathed in red lighting and we
see **THEDA** and **GIRL** again.

THEDA: green is the healing
he allus said, green is the healing...
I kin hear him now, honey
so rich as that talkin was
and fine, like burgundy,
honey, fine wine and so pretty,
that man's color was burgundy
like the street I lived on back when--
if I could, if I knew the way
to be writin' him up, or paintin' that time for you,
he'd be burgundy.....yeah, the burgundy letters
with all my lovin'
I ain't found any like him
but i keep going--
(tone changes to irritation)
In a city like this, chile
it's the strong preyin' on the weak
stompin' down the competition
and mens ornery
if you want some body at yo throat
get yourself a mean dog
Go on home, baby, go on home!
(mellower tone)
How can i tell you a thing!

I keep followin that sun
hopin it'll dry out these old bones
from what's jumped on 'em
to make 'em grow the way they do
then I'll get ovah and there'll be
paradise for sure
shinin' like sunday mornin'

THEDA reaches under the table for her large carpetbag filled with stuff. She places it on the table, adds cigarettes and her small purse to it. She turns to the **GIRL** who is gathering her recording equipment:

Evenin' chile…will ya walk an old woman down…take a cig...for the road.

GIRL does accept the offer this time, smiling, as if she knows she is giving Theda the gift of accepting her offer even though she doesn't smoke. She offers Theda her arm. **Theda** hooks arms, places her bag lightly in the crook of the other arm and they exit to harmonica blues. Lights fade to black.
HECTOR is left alone in the violet light, mythic in proportion, as the music dies and we hear the steps fading into the distance.

THIS IS IT!

THE MIRACLE OF WHY WE'RE HERE
for George Houston Bass, who knew, inspired, loved....

SETTING: NEW BEDFORD WATERFRONT

CHARACTERS:
JAMES
MARGO
JESSIE
THE VOICE
DANCER/MIME
CHORUS

The performance area is ideally an arena stage which allows
entry from different vantage points. There is scaffolding on the
upper west side which serves as the "upper room" and also as
the roof of the world below it. The ladder to the top will be used
by characters as they ascend and descend between levels of
reality.
Prominent on one side of the scaffold is an intercom which serves
as a virtual character. It must be defined as a player and this
can be done by spotlighting it at the beginning of Act I.

James--a tall, rugged mariner who evokes the waterfront with
its rugged demands and distinct lifestyle.
He is 32, black, originally from the South, transplanted
North by economic need. He moves slowly and surely,
has a definite stance, speaks little, listening to others refer to him
in the third person, objectively disengaged. He is a hard
worker and yet finds it equally difficult to get ahead in this
environment.

Margo--average in every way, a flexible, empathetic bartender
who evokes the displaced persona of a woman who followed
the path life presented--she is unsatisfied but reasonably happy
in her unglamorous spot-she is in her 40's, of Franco-American
background, a divorced mother of two with a Portuguese boyfriend.
She is other-directed and often uses the second person to

implicate others in her point of view. She looks directly out to the audience or up to God using the same smile as punctuation along the way. She is quick in recalling the past and her voice follows the same tempo.

Jessie--an energetic adolescent-mobile, a bit scattered, with a collection of friends and of objects of desire. She lives independently with her mother in her own space and entertains friends and dreams. She is Cape Verdean and her multicultural roots are revealed in her fondness for exotic cultures. She is fluid and moves like a dancer about the stage. She is free.

The Dancer/Mime--a harlequin in motley who moves in between the speech

The Chorus--Lady in a Rocking Chair; Boy with Skateboard; Man on the Corner; Girl with Headset

The Cast can be robed simply in short tunics and tights of uniform color or varied tones. This will allow the audience to focus on words and promote freedom of movement. It will also underscore the allegorical nature and timeless quality of the drama.

The Chorus should have props suitable to their position--eg., man can lean on mailbox, lady can sew, etc. Props are minimal since the poetics is conveyed in image and sound. They should, however, reflect the working class scene.

ACT I

SCENE I

from offstage a **Voice** announces:
THE OUTLAWED—JAMES

VOICE comes over intercom announcing James in presence and intention:
He was James of the motorcycle, James of the false teeth
James whose bite has been cut by thirty-two years of passing
through. James of migrations holding on to the word "no",
isolating everything that would bind him to one place.
He says ...

JAMES : (enters slowly) Every time I see a bus
I wanna get on it
It's hard to get next to the truth

VOICE: he learned these words in Boston, clipped
staccato like the person who taught him
their usefulness

JAMES: "T" man he was a friend, and a port-in-
a-storm, he took me home
to Mission Hill, wasn't more than a
nest with crates for tables and pizza
and beer, but up from Alabama
with a sack of clothes and my brother's
watch--Younger's timepiece--well, it
was the best, a life saver-
(he looks at the pocket watch, bleary-faced from age)

VOICE: Younger, who rolled and knifed a drunk
for drug money, who seized out from drinking
'til he blacked out, too frail to do the time..

JAMES: Younger, whose place I took on the chain gang

quitting the loading dock where I'd come up since
I was ten for hard labor in red clay—

MAN ON CORNER: James of the leathered neck, he'd
lay out miles of pipe with that 6 foot,
bent-back, trowel-wide hands

JAMES: I loved the southland the way you love a woman
when she's run to seed, because she had the
raw warmth

WOMAN IN CHAIR: James of the frayed, puckered touch-
he'd stroke you with fingertips of those
huge, water-marked hands he used to scrub
tiles over and over...

BOY: James who left Alabama with only a sack of
clothes for Boston...comin' in to Trailways
drinkin whiskey in the gazebo
on the Common and finding "T"

GIRL: and finding the letter from Younger at
Sid's Lunch-and Sid the only one he knew
from home-

JAMES: Younger signed only with an "x", so
I knew he got help-turns out, Lou
was his wife and could write and they
owned a packy in Birmingham now--he
was sellin and not partakin—

MAN: that James came from farmers
and when he got that news, he said
never mind all that and moved on

JAMES: I don't want to get by...but get ovah

WOMAN: they called him the "Doctor" yes,
because he could right the wrong
because he'd find the place in your skin

where what you craved would go in
and you'd never feel pain--he worked over
people with the stuff in his bags

MAN:
that James, he can work ya over
with those hammers of hands

JAMES: I've been travelin'
out of one big bag for the last twelve years
in perpetual motion--always with my
ticket, always with my running shoes
my Gibson--I hear delta, hear bop,
hearing jazz, fretting up and down
the neck only for those who run cool
at night
smokin'

GIRL: James who is the instrument

BOY: James who broke up fights wherever he played
he smells of leather, saddle soap, cooking oil-he
can do it all!

JAMES: I just wanted a night that would let me shine
without anything in my hand--I went from city
to city looking for that night-

WOMAN: He has no souvenirs, no receipts, menus,
stolen glasses, women's numbers...
I heard he went back to Philly and found
the woman gone and a paternity suit
on the table...his memory lasts no longer
than last night and he says...

JAMES: Everytime I see a woman, I wanna get on it
It's hard to live up to the truth

GIRL: He says he likes to enter different worlds!

BOY: He traveled America on the $99.00 special,
looking for a ranch to wash his rope-cut hands!

WOMAN: His daughter lies alone while her young mother
works on an Alzheimer ward in Boston.

JAMES: I came to New Bedford, a city of
immigrants in the elbow of Massachusetts that
reaches toward the ocean. I came into
the flow of people who brought to the city
its flavor of island and sea, Cape Verdean and
then Portuguese whalemen and sailors who
risked their lives each day and named
their boats after daughters for grace and
protection: the Tina, the Angela, the Jenny--
New Bedford of Americans of color looking for a
town with heart, of disinherited pockets of
musicians fighting for survival and
city grants--New Bedford, that gateway transit
on the edge of the ocean, that held its people
like flowers in an international garden:
Latin zinnias, Greek and Lebanese cyclamen,
African violets--each needing its own particular
nourishment and identifying it as the same,
common soil.

GIRL: New Bedford of the smokestacks, spires, masts funneling
the industry and dreams of the people
above the skyline.

BOY: New Bedford of the waterfront whose planks
tapped out the rhythm of bodies heavy as sacks of fish!

MAN: New Bedford of the dockside watering holes that
would wash away the odor of cut cod.

WOMAN: New Bedford of the still-lit gaslights that illumine a city
made rich on whale oil lighting lamps in panamerican
nights.

JAMES: New Bedford whose humility and hospitality,
whose supermarket lines, lines of churches,
lines of men sloughing off tons of fillets a week
would keep me here.
New Bedford of the shuttling loom, the frozen wage,
the shrouded-black, middle-aged grandmothers
kneading breads of the old country with grandkids
in lurex and law school--
New Bedford rising from its knees in the mix
of tongues striving to make it home
New Bedford offering an address for the room
in the sky-blue house on the rainbow block
of two-storied tenements with stone saint statues
walled in the vegetable gardens.

ALL: New Bedford--there are those who call it home!

Scene 1 closes with music of area (Portuguese or
Creole song, upbeat)

SCENE II

MARGO
Margo enters from the south side and proceeds to the scaffold
which she uses as a bar counter. She places a bottle and some
glasses on it along with a small bar towel. She will use these
props at intervals throughout her monologue. She has used
make-up and some jewelry to accent her "femininity" and it
is this trait she will convey in her speech.

MARGO: You know, dressing in denim and eyeliner helps
keep you young. Even though you are older
you are no less limber, weighing in at the same
place, feeling heavier since you're more satisfied.
You work like the rest in your town--
when they dress in uniforms white, black, or blue
you pick one up and do that, too-and
you serve people but even then you try
to maintain yourself. You can pick a brooch or

a pair of earrings, say, to make your day.
You know, rubbing that counter in the same spots
and erasing the wet glass rings sure is tiresome--
'specially if you come from lobsterin' with your man.
And you just know that every fool who asks you
for a dime to call his mother is bound
to get your stock reply: I've only got 2 cents
and some aspirin--
You have to keep a lil' surprise in life and that's
tough enough--and when you've got two kids,
and they're spit images of each other, well
that's double your trouble. You wish
you had an answer for the times when someone says,
"I think I'm losing my mind!"
'cos you want to say "I've been wanting to do that
for a week!" You stop reading the newspaper,
or watching t.v., feeling that hard copy
keeps folks' heads between their legs--
and you got the kids to consider. You know
that being a mother lasts--and a man might leave
again, since he's repeated that tune before.

WOMAN: (walking in from the north side, working her
way to the other side of the "bar")
Even though you want the golden ring, honey,
and you believe it, you truly do, you won't be
moved-moving takes money for the passage
and you don't have enough in tips
to rearrange your make-up.

MARGO: You know, you can't afford to drop even a dime
on yourself and so punch in and out every day.
You may work in a bar and not use a time clock
but you time yourself by the clientele. You know
if the bar is in New Beige the customers
might not be understood in English and
the ones there at 3 AM won't be able to be
understood at all--before you leave home
you say a prayer that all knives stay in pockets
and all stories follow the same formula

so you'll know what to say--when you get there
you mix a whiskey sour and think about something
that will give you strength to pass through-
you might think of that old man of yours
the one you met the Center St. fair over cider
and fiddle tunes, the one who took you up
to the Elks to hear some bottomed-out
sounds that reminded you of the Fatha' Hines
record your dad hid from you when you
were a kid.

MAN: (entering form the north)
You might think on that man too long and get to
wonderin' when he's gonna come back for the
third time with what all, another finger lost
to one of them cutting winches

GIRL: (entering from south) It might be better to picture yourself
as somebody
you'd like to be: a wonderful woman with guts and
beauty, too--a cross between Kate Hepburn and
those nuns with faraway eyes you helped
to punch out communion hosts from long wafer
sheets when you were a girl.

BOY: (climbing scaffold, following girl)
You know you need role models--you don't
have much family left, and even the women
you know are nasty-mouthed, smelling of semen
and gin or swaggering in with shirts
advertising "ugly mean and nasty"
and their fillet-knife-carrying girlfriends'
initials tattooed on their arms in blueblack
ink

MARGO: (wiping the counter down, looking out at
audience with attitude that she has heard the advice of the visitors)
You love them, you love them, that's what
Father Adrian kept saying as he took Polaroids
in the chapel's gift shop-and he heard the

confession quickly and in the moments of
penance which were moments of peace
you knew it was true--even as they laugh
and steal small change from the register to
play favorites from the jukebox--"islands
in the stream", that's got to be a favorite-
Cindy, a reg'lar and tough as a hammerhead
on a nail will punch it in, leaving you free
to keep an ear out for the sounds folks make
to say where the city's going: how the place
has gotta be changin' when the son known
all-over-the-block got himself a movie, when
the crazy painter is selling in new york, and when
the pool-ace-junkie is a priest now in Boston
street life

MAN: You know you need something---sure,
you were raised by a mother who forgot
her French as the city changed its complexion
but still called you "Margot" for its effect –
you may have been raised by a father who came
to New England to work in the mills and
survived on cold pork and hot potatoes
sounding out grace before every meal--you know

they were nervous of god and neighbors
and whispered their conversations behind
closed doors, mumbled as prayers-every night
you said the rosary together after mother lit
the votive candle. The hour it took was irretrievable
and you know it held you together.

WOMAN: You may remember how you could walk upstairs
as a young girl, past them with paper bag-covered
books whose contents go unused now.
You hear your mother's "You look so pretty"
as a blessing not a vanity.

MARGO: You may think about some fantastic place
where you planned to live, a place like

Four Corners where there was country
and flowers and no gossip and a horse
with a wild mane you could ride--this place
was in the south and the women there strolled
and smiled in gardens. The only things about it
and the Atlantic bar was that they both served soup
and had friendly men for cooks. You know,
you might remember this when you pick a stool
for yourself and swivel on it waiting for him
to serve you. It'll be just a short while, relax,
honey, you really don't have to do it all
yourself, you know....

Music to fill time/space in place of dialogue as **Scene II closes.**
with a tune one would likely find on the jukebox would work----
pop, country, r&b.

SCENE III
Light shines onto the east entry of the arena to illumine Jessie's
path. She traipses in delighted to be here, confronting the
audience and her surroundings. She is the first character to
do so.

JESSIE: I know more than you might think.
I've heard plenty and I've seen more than
people say. Not that I'd repeat it-but
I'd like to say something about myself-
I figure it's about that time. I'm seventeen
now and people here think I'm out-of-the-
ordinary or out of sorts, or "different"-
they don't like what they call my "lifestyle"
in the small, shingled cabin I built in the back
of my mom's-even tho' they had four years
to get used to it! they don't approve of what
I put on my back--Madewell overalls and shirts
from ma's factory--think it's not "ladylike"
not to mention my hair! they laughed at me
in school because I questioned everything, and
in church likewise and more so, so I haven't
seen a blue book since I was fifteen-I have

---

nobody to worry about except ma and she
pretty well takes care of herself. She brings home
enough for two and spends her time home, 'cept
when she's under the influence of a coupla beers
or some man, and never minds me. I live by myself
on that small lot sandwiched in between the ranches
and what used to be the Poor Farm.

GIRL: (skipping into the arena) People in New Bedford think Jessie's
weird, but I think she's cool. I wish I didn't
have to go to my boring school...!

BOY: (comes out on skateboard) I used to skateboard past there
to check her cabin out--she helped me with my Spanish
and even gave me a taste of wine!

MAN: (enters with pool cue) That girl is as smart as a boy! They gave
her a job sweepin' the Atlantic Bar, and she
beat me at pool...I call her "pockets" 'cos
she can call 'em!

WOMAN: (enters in apron) She gave me a recipe for chowder
 I'd never tried, and hot peppers from her garden
to keep us satisfied all summer--she cooks
for the bar and Margo's kids, she's a whiz..

JESSIE: I learned a lot coming up here. I'm not a hermit
at all-I get around, see plenty of people: ma's
stitchin' buddies, folks from the Atlantic, the old
folkies from Tryworks coffeehouse...now that it's
gone, they play on the wall at East Beach, I strum
along with Con when he gets down, and my pals
Roy and Boo, they've been places and can tell
how it's like to live with moccasins or wooden shoes
or none. At their place across the river I
can walk in and say whatever or just watch
light on the stained glass window Roy made-Joe
comes by with lobsters and we'll drive to Eric's
jungle apartment where he performs surgery
on my hair so I look like Jolly Rog, his parrot, in my

fine plumage! I got a life.....
When I come home, it comes undone.

(she turns and looks around at the stage which
has been decorated with exotic stuff: masks, coral,
cultural icons)

This must be a strange sight to you--everything
hanging off the walls--like a spirit house or
a woman's house. I thought it would be
a good way to expose what I could do. People bring
me little gifts, too, but I ask them to leave their gossip
at the door. There's no one around like that right now
but I only feel it on winter nights when nobody comes by.
There's been a string of them lately. It's cold in this
place with only a little Glenwood to heat it but
my longjohns are woolly! I don't get fooled by the suit
of clothes myself. Some people, their clothes gets in the way
of a natural line. Some imitate what they're looking for.
 I always wonder if people will wear clothes to
match their words or find words to match their clothes.
It's a scream!
I only have one item I like, this little star I wear
on my vest..(she fondles it)
just once I'd like to have something I'd care about
losing…so I wouldn't think "I've done this to death"-
it's a mighty small world if loss devastates you, but
I'd like to wake up one day having something
that means that much, the world to me...

WOMAN : they sent her to the clinic once
for an eval., and Mo, the worker who blows
sax at the Bomb on Sundays, wrote the only
thing off- kilter was she might "frighten her peers"-

She's gotta learn to shut her mouth,
and look less like a missing link-at
least her hair ain't pink!

JESSIE: It's just 'cos I don't represent-- my

attitude ain't black or white,
my hair, talk, and clothes change
with what I like
at the time, but that's fine
with me--see my icon on the wall
it's from some other culture-what I love
are the head dresses of colors and feathers-
It seems these people were respected
they live far from here, far from cities
with people obese and opaque with status, far
from the nuclear fallout that threatens
my city, far from the toxic waste here
the high pcb's in the river...hey, this isn't
fiction, it's mother earth news talking,
I'm telling you, these people are out
browned and shining by sunlight or something
transparent...I want to be one of them!
I own only one book, an art book-I believe
it'll help me see-I'm going into this thing
whole-souled, so I'm bound to pick it up and
when I'm done it'll carry me
like knowledge, like something written in stone,
like the train that still transports near here,
whistling down the night with long, held notes
saying "one train, one train, get on it and ride"

blues harp plays as we **fade out on ACT 1**

ACT II

SCENE I

DANCER: enters from the east and moves in diverse
directions to jazz passages-an expansive
movement throughout the arena to reggae and
calypso--the mood is an evocative rendering of
the past and an embrace of what can be--as
the dance progresses, lights slowly reveal the
"upper room" . There is a rocker there...
As the old French lullaby is sung, the mime
steps lightly to the upper room as if rising to

heaven and/or a higher state of being...

VOICE: there was an upper room, one in the far
recesses of the house, there was light
falling on the ample rocker where a woman
sat with a girl. The woman is dressed in faille
or shantung and the girl is in a pastel romper-she
is playing with beads around the woman's
neck. They might be rosary beads or worry
beads or mardi gras beads yet the child
tosses her head like a young foal. The woman
is singing to her and it's such a sweet voice
from such a strong woman:
"P'tit Jesus, Bonjour
mes delices, mes delices
P'tit jesus, Bonjour
mes delices et mes amours
J'ai reve cette nuit
Que j'etais en Paradis (2 times)
avec les anges"

CHORUS: (entering from diverse directions in turn):

BOY: this is the song the aunt sang
MAN: this is the song Aunt Ida sang to me
GIRL: this is the song she was given by her father
when she was my age
WOMAN: this is the song of the ancestors
ALL: this is becoming the song of the child

DANCER: raises arms heavenward-drops them to her side
in unison with the Chorus' lines:
CHORUS: raise that baby (loudly) (upward motion)
lay that baby to rest (softer) (falling motion)

lights fall off and then darkness

SCENE 2
Stage is lit to suggest dusk in winter. A moon is hung from
the scaffold as a suggestive prop.

JAMES: (enters from the north, moving as if treading
snow, watching his steps on the ground)
When you make footprints in the snow you leave
tracks larger than your feet
hoping those huge impressions scare anybody
who dares follow--
this is the path of industry, of waterfront
processing plants unwinding south, of money...

MARGO: (enters from the south, slouching along looking
for something as though she is lost)
You came to it walking along shoulders slumped,
head bent in one direction that happens to be
down, eyeing a course littered with rubble and
shards of broken glass as fractured and
variegated as pieces of the heart. You can be
sure it was the path of least resistance.

JESSIE: (enters from the east, looking outward, future directed
and enthusiastically hopeful):
the path of the meridians--it sounded like something
put together because it was true and sounded right
it's something about degrees and distances, about
how we follow the same line--either from pole
to pole or sea to sea--it connects bodies-it
connects places and time doesn't matter.
You may have sunrise over some beach and
people waiting to watch it appear behind a hill
somewhere else. These places may look
different--one has palms blowing,
another has drought, but they are together
on the path like a wavelength—

JAMES: Do right, do right--no time to talk to
Strawberry and hang on his houseboat-no
quick pivot into the Estoril
for an espresso with Kahlua to lace it
and the night up right--this was a night

different from all others-the night my ship
comes in! the night the Ecuador came
through haulin' lumber for urban renewal
and a cargo of bitter herb and dope
to keep 'em hoppin' 'til they remembered
nothin'--do right, do right-I can't see
how far I've come, but know where I'm goin'

MARGO:
this night would be unlike others-who could tell
how long this would take? the reunion with Les,
the tears, the sweet, sweet touch-You had told
nobody-never mind that les had lost
another finger to a winch-never mind that money
was swallowed up in his drinking-you hope
nobody mistakes the Ecuador for a vessel
out of New Bedford and takes pot-shots
at the men-You feel something strange
where your gut should be when you think of Les and
so think of the kids with memère tonight
how tired they were of beans and rice diets,
how you couldn't afford the Sunday morning
treats any more—

JESSIE: This night is different all right--Lately, I've been
following the equator reading about lost
tribes and practicing Spanish with that barfly Jose
It's stayed in me like an attitude
where all lines come full circle
and the territory is mapped
telling me how far I've come tonight,
I'll taste Ecuador!
I plan to see the ship arrive: I know
how it rounds the beach near the old fort,
creeps past the lighthouse to the harbor
and piers. It'll dock behind Strawberry's
boat, like a lion and mouse in the same bunk!
Strawberry'll come out in house slippers
and blink the snow out of his eyes--Ecuador
here! I've wanted to see that forever!

Margo and Jessie exit though their respective directions.

JAMES: You know, the old underground, that tunnel
to the sea that had run slaves to freedom
and run rum and now run me, James (he hits
his chest), to the promise of freedom as a man
'stead of hands-for-hire. Get a move on,
yeh, there's the old fort fronting the ocean,
the crest of beach outlined in those rocks
piled like a testimonial to an unknown god.
somewhere ahead must be the fringe of grass
covering the entrance to the passage back--back
to the known god, money, a man
named Ben and 3 am-once the goods are
delivered it'd be set. It's all waiting--
and I'm gonna use it!

MARGO: (enters from the south)
Between a rock and hard time with no anchor
to hug, you can see Les as an option-you can see
yourself in hard places with Les, walking past
these neighborhoods without windows and with signs
advertising long names that resounded
like long knives whistling through air
when you sounded them out: Rincón
Angél, Casa Creole, Borinquen. A mile of grit
heading to the fort--you draw your hood
over your head and cast shadow like a monk.
It doesn't keep the acid-odor from the factory
away--it becomes breath--and you think of Les'
soles smelling of cut cod always--God, New
Bedford--it's not a human smell-you're grateful
it tastes anyway, of salt cod and quahogs and
mussel stew--and grateful that you remember
this when you run along the rocks and empty
shells that cross the sea.

JESSIE: (enters from the east)
the smoke from the nightsky ahead is a milestone

and a call--I raise my knees to my chest almost
when I get excited and I feel ready now!
I want my red boots to mark the snow like scarlet
suns! I see a short hill ahead-steep, with plenty
of scrub to hang onto for balance.
I see muscled men who'll enter this world,
waving foreign hellos against my hard-edged night.
Despite snow falling thick as the lace my grandmother
tats on handkerchiefs, I see the frame
of their ship, their lanterns like beacons and
the rope and rigging that keep them from
drowning.

lights fade-characters bow their heads as they leave stage

SCENE III
The stage has been transformed. There is now a tubular tunnel
at the foot of the scaffolding. Graffiti reading "Rock Force"
and "South First Posse" are on the "walls".

JAMES: (approaches foot of tunnel, reaches in and removes
bag of powdery stuff (suggests hard drugs), checks
it to make sure contents are right)
They sell drugs the way their fathers sold slaves.
That's soon gonna change...when my ship come
in. Gettin' a little satisfaction' tonight!
(He begins to sing as he goes through ritual
enactment of filling his pipe and smoking as he
walks away)

JESSIE: (Yells loudly as she falls into tunnel)
AAAAAAAAaaaaaaaaaaaaaa!

JAMES: What the devil?
(looks in direction of tunnel where yell has
come from, out to see for his ship)
Ain't time yet! Got time.....

(runs back to tunnel, loses bag on way--sees
Jessie prone-she's fallen in with one arm sticking out

149

of tunnel, tries to drag her out, but can't—
he must enter tunnel and dislodge her—he goes in, dislodges her and
brings her to tunnel entry -begins to apply lifesaving techniques and
she finally breathes again)

JESSIE: I wanna know who all these people are...
JAMES: What?
JESSIE: Who are they?
JAMES: Who are you?
JESSIE: Where am I? It's so cold.
(he wraps her in his coat)
JESSIE: I came here without a coat and I'm
leavin' with one!
JAMES: (looks at her old sweatshirt with the name
of an Ivy League school)
Now, baby, stop complainin'...you got a coat
on your back all right...you must've got lost somewhere.
JESSIE: Where are the island people?
JAMES: The island people..
JESSIE: The island people--I've lived through people
who've come from islands, lived off islands...and
they're not here.
JAMES: It's cold here.
JESSIE: I can tell that! How are we gettin' out of this fix
is the question.
JAMES: Fix. Yeah, that is the question. Honeylamb,
I gotta be movin out soon.

JESSIE: If I been to the islands I could've woven us a
ladder of moss and we'd be out in no time!
JAMES: (confused by her incoherent speech)
Are you a weaver or artist or somethin'?
JESSIE: My mother is Cape Verdean. If I were there,
or off the coast of Africa somewhere or
where they can dance around obstacles all day
I'd know what to do. I fell off the mound..
I'm confused. We're stuck here
and now...
JAMES: Yeh, one step ahead of suicide...You'll be checkin'

out the latinos tomorrow, kiddo. The boat's
comin' in.
JESSIE: It's out there now. I came here to see it.
I mean to find out what they're up to
and if I can help
JAMES: It's gone by...b'lieve me.
JESSIE: What was it like? I figured from the smoke
it must be huge-
JAMES: (evasively) I didn't notice...
JESSIE: I remember what those poets said about the moonflowers,
the toucans, their call is fixed in me..
JAMES: You're too much! I know my own name...and that's
enough!
JESSIE: I'm Jessie. Is that all?....Hey, I know you...you work
for Vinnie...he always said you can haul more than
anybody he'd seen at Fulton St.
JAMES: Mebbe....
JESSIE: You're not much of a talker--it's like you're
in a hurry to get somewhere..
JAMES: I was....I am

James and Jessie realize at the same time
that a huge mound of earth was dislodged from
the roof of the tunnel when he entered to move her.
It now blocks their path.

JESSIE: I can stand on your shoulders and run for help!
JAMES: Let me think this through..
JESSIE: (realizing he is slow and deliberate)
We could die waiting for you to figure it out..
They try her plan yet she fails to stay balanced.
JESSIE: (angry) What the hell do you know?
JAMES: I know the ways of the seasons, the colors of the
seasons, the keys and the codes. I know how to
tune an instrument to the right key and the code of
flags they use at sea.
JESSIE: Do you know the distress signal?

They huddle closer, listening to the music blaring from the
Ecuador.

JESSIE: Is that real?
JAMES: That's the language of drums. Don't interrupt it.
That's a conversation.
JESSIE: What are they saying?
JAMES:
They're sayin' young ladies should be still
and quiet if marryin' s their will-
JESSIE: I wanna work my way up to myself. To tell
you the truth, if the trip has to be a journey in
hell, I'd rather not have money for the fare.
but I like you, what's-your-name-
JAMES: I am James. I'd rather make my exit.
They hear footsteps and listen to sounds above on
the scaffolding.
JESSIE: Check that...doesn't sound like a badger
to me.
(she yells out) Ayuda, ayuda..
(turns to James) just in case they're Spanish!

Margo peers down from her perch above them.
MARGO: What's going on? (recognizing them both)
Why , honey, how do you happen to be here..?
JAMES: Do something!
MARGO: What *can I* do?
JAMES: You're asking us? Can't you see a way?
MARGO: I barely picked my way down ..thought I might
see Les from here.

JAMES: Why do you want to see Les?
JESSIE: Les is her old man.
(aside to James) that's a good question.
MARGO: I'm lookin'....wait a minute!
She disappears from view.
JAMES: The possibilities are endless in anticipating our end!
JESSIE: That's Margo from the Atlantic. Don't worry.
She's sharp...she'll find a way to make do. She
always does.

Margo returns with a cast-off rope from the beach.

MARGO:
I found it on the beach. Grab an end!
JAMES: That's a lifeline, girl!

They climb over the obstacle. Margo is still above them.

JAMES: Will you come down to our level so we can thank you?
MARGO: I got a rendezvous with a man...can't...
JAMES: I'm a man who's just gotta thank you...for helpin' this child.
JESSIE: speak for yourself...
MARGO: I know you, you're James, the one they call James the hands...you never take nuthin from nobody..
JAMES: That's what they say?

JESSIE: That's what they say...go ahead, let her teach you the difference between a golddigger and an alchemist.

JAMES: What's an alch---hey, your eyes are deep as a grave. What'd you see?

JESSIE: You ...and me....and her...like a family.
MARGO: No! Jessie, he's a master of the ropes-but whether it's a woman or a horse, it's all the same to him, he just wants to rope it in....No way!
JESSIE: Margo, I was gone! I was out and he brought me back! and this is the first time I've known you not to be watching, dressed for the occasion...You did it!
MARGO: I was happy to do it. Anybody could have done it.
JAMES: but it was you....you took a part...you had to do it.
MARGO: I feel like I got an invitation to the human race.
JAMES: Me, too. I've been trying to be ahead of my time. I may need to do some time soon...there's a man I was 'spozed to meet, he'll likely set me up..
MARGO: You can come to my place...nobody will know.. you, too, Jes'
JESSIE: Well, thanks, I got meatpies and beer. I'll

build you a house of cards or clean your pockets
playin' them out.

JAMES: Girl, shut up! We'll feed you!

MARGO: I'm cookin'!
ALL: Let's do it!

they link arms together as chorus comes out

CHORUS: this is the song we all sing
this is the song of the room
this is the song of the room rocking
this is the song of the room rocking red

JAMES: sometimes we get what we deserve
JESSIE: sometimes we get what we expect
MARGO: sometimes we find our true faces and names
DANCER: moves joyously and now is no longer a mime
but has a voice, joining others in:

ALL: Navaho Song:
In beauty I walk
with delight before me I walk
with beauty behind me I walk
with beauty above and about me I walk
It is finished in delight
It is finished in beauty
It is finished in beauty